She Had No Business

Dear Erin,

May you remember your mother's strength and continue to have "No Business" being a spunky and strong women the way she was!

Much Love,
Jessica
xo

God Bless!

May you continue to grow, use
your talents to love the
and "caring" Person, Shirley
Brings. Person Shirley
and should Nemani

Martin was.

Love, Jozie
X

She Had No Business

a real life tale
of faith, courage,
and beating the odds

JESSICA VARIAN CARROLL

inspired girl BOOKS

To Jared, Noah, Reilly, and Damian – just remember
all things are possible…

"Jessica is an absolutely amazing and multifaceted woman. She will try her hardest to help you with anything you ask of her and more all while running a successful business, raising children, and still having time for friends. I honestly don't know how she does it. She brings so much joy to any space she walks in!"

~ Kirsten Seidle Gizzi

"Jessica is an infectious and unstoppable force of positivity, compassion, and miracle making. Her words will mobilize the faith you need to make your dreams come true and make you laugh spastically while doing it."

~ Dr. Veera Gupta

"Jessica is a successful, strong, independent woman who lifts up others & cheers them on by inspiring them to follow their dreams. Her support & encouragement is contagious. Jessica has a positive vibe that connects women together feeling empowered by one another."

~ Marianne Peluso

"This isn't a book of hyperbole; Jessica is the real deal. Her stories will ring true as she shares insight culled from balancing her growing, successful business, her semi-annual women's conferences that she co-created and co-orchestrated and her large family that she's raising on her own as a single mom. With a can-do attitude, wit and genuine warmth and compassion for others, she's a beacon for all who are looking for a bit of light in how to proceed forward with their life."

~ Bob Ellis

"Jessica is a true source of light to everyone she meets and encourages women to reach for the stars! Her infectious passion to support other women—through her SOAR events and charity work—comes from a genuine place in her heart, inspiring everyone to reach higher and strive to be the best version of themselves."

~ Carey Balogh

Contents

Hey there, Sunshine,

Have you ever felt like you are doing something you have no business doing? Have you ever not done something because you thought, *who am I* to do that?

Well, I get it. I have no business writing a book, but you better believe I'm doing it anyway! And let me tell you, if you've been on this ride with me, you know you will be in here somewhere.

Wow, I can't believe there is a big cover with a fancy picture of me on the front and the most amazing kind words from people I adore on the back and bits and pieces of my story on the pages in between. And you are here, right along with me. So yeah, if you're reading this (in which I believe you are), that means I have done it. I have written a book, my very own book. Let me explain a little on how we got here and by the way, thank you so much for picking up a copy and reading it.

My dear friend, business partner, and published author Jenn Tuma-Young said to me out of the blue that she'd like to take on a new client and help them write a book, guide them along the way, through the ins and outs of the publishing world. So if you know me I went right into action to help her land that dream client. I made a list of people who I thought would want to write a book or who would have a great story to share. Immediately I whipped up a quick text and shot it out to some dear friends Natalie, Carey, & Bob. Never thinking for even just one moment "what about me?". You see, it never really is about me. I always think of others before myself, and I'm totally okay with that. If I can make something happen for other people then that my friend is a blessing in itself. That's why it's so wild that my photo, me dolled up and all by myself, is on the cover of this book.

And a little story about that by the way. It was no coincidence that I got my final cover back on the morning of Independence Day. I looked at it and said heck yeah to that independent woman on the cover, even though I don't always feel like her. One of the things I've learned when getting photos done is that posture is everything!! I'm not going to lie, when I first saw the pictures, I wasn't happy with how I looked. Then I saw the one photo we chose for the cover. I was standing tall and it not only changed the look of the photos, it changed the way I felt about myself. Confidence is everything! So don't shy away from the camera—embrace it! Throw your shoulders back, hold your head high, and good lighting doesn't hurt. I think every woman needs to get professional photos done at least once in their lives! "Giselle, who?!" You are just as amazing inside and out!

Sorry I digressed a bit, but I had to get that out of my system! Anyhow, the whole idea of writing this book kept swirling in my head for some reason. At that time I felt I kind of hit a plateau personally and professionally. I felt like I was capable of more, but I was standing in my own way, and I wasn't quite sure how or why? I've always known I surely had things from my past that I hadn't fully acknowledged or dealt with, so maybe that was what was holding me back? I figured maybe just maybe if I took the time to really process, write, and go through all these things maybe that would help? I'm the type of person that always looks forward, not back. Things are behind us for a reason right? So many crappy things I've had to go through, why would I want to think about those things ever again? Plus I did actually know that I had a book inside of me—the title already came to me a few months prior in the middle of the night.

So a few hours later after Jenn and I had spoken, I mustered the courage to ask Jenn what she thought about me writing the book? I mean I haven't made a million dollars, I didn't rescue orphan giraffes from a jungle, I really don't always have it all together... I'm just simple old me but I have had many experiences and maybe it would help me to share them. Maybe it would help women like me find their own faith and courage during challenging times. Maybe it would help even just one woman dream bigger, break out of the mold, and go for it. So I put it out there.

Jenn immediately said YES, and she got full on goose bumps. It was meant to be. She could feel it. After all, can you believe the reason we even connected over coffee way back in 2013 was because I wanted to write a book?! Six years and a bond stronger than ever—we both knew it was time. Her mind immediately went into action like "popcorn" as she referred to it. She had so many ideas.

Now mind you, I didn't want Jenn to do me a favor. I knew this was her livelihood, and she was looking for a new client. I made it clear that I wanted to work with her, as a real client. She would help me draw stories out of my heart and we would spend 6 months navigating it all, figuring out the structure of the book and choosing which path to publication would be best. This would be a major investment, in both time and money—one of my biggest that would be spent purely on myself. I've never spent that kind of money, like ever, unless it was a car or something like that where it would be for the family and business. I decided I was worth it. I would do it. I deserved it. I would be helping myself and it would be a bonus if I could help just one reader get through something, anything. So here we are just a few months later the writing is done, all 40,000 words. I did it and Jenn was instrumental in the process.

A Memoir, But Not Really a Memoir: A Note About the Structure of the Book

So while this book shares so many stories from my life, it's not in sequential order front to back. It is more like vignettes with short stories around topics that were important for me to share with you. Picture the book to have 3 sections: section 1 dives into celebrating who we are, section 2 is all about finding your calling, and section 3 is dedicated to helping others. I hope you see yourself in my stories and you take actions in your life to really bust out and beat all the odds! I know with my whole heart you can and will do the most extraordinary things. I can't wait to hear all about them in your very own book!

xo,
Me

Section 1

Celebrating Who We Are

"I had no business celebrating my birthday, I wasn't even supposed to be born...but I found my tribe, made it a tradition, and did it anyway!"

CHAPTER
One

Going from Backstage to Front and Center

"The more you praise and celebrate your life, the more there is in life to celebrate."
~ Oprah Winfrey

Every year I throw myself a big birthday celebration. Kind of funny I should celebrate my birth this way, I wasn't even supposed to be born. My mom was just sixteen when she had me. Talk about a turnaround.

But I think that's part of the deal, you don't get to plan everything in life. We all get thrown curveballs whether it be from choices we made or just the Universe giving us a surprise. Some surprises are good, and some just plain stink. And so, some things should definitely be planned, like a birthday party. Not just because it's fun, but also because it sends a signal to the world—I matter and some of the unplanned things can truly be the best gifts.

I'll tell you more about my birth story later. It's a doozy of a beginning, that's for sure. But the fact is for most of my life I was more of a "behind the scenes, no need to focus on me, divert the attention" kind of girl. And with that, I began to love throwing parties for other people, just not myself.

Catering to Everyone But Me

I was known as "Jessica the Hostess with the Mostess" as my family called me or "Jessica Messica" as my father would say. I think he just liked the sound of it because, of course, that could never be true not with my need for neatness even back then! I mean, in the third grade I stayed in from recess to organize Mrs. Kocen's bookshelf at Wanamassa School. In fifth grade I went over to my friend Mhairi's house and I organized her whole closet (her mother was blown away by the way). Jessica Messica? No way.

So, which nickname do you think I would prefer? I took on the Hostess with the Mostess title with pride. Heck yeah! From very early on when my family would get together for one reason or another, my Aunt Michele would suggest things for me to do like pass the pizza bagels, grab some plates, even as a child I was always the one pitching in at parties. And then there was my Aunt Sandy whose unique attention to detail just topped the charts. With her computer printed banners that you had to color in—gotta love the early eighties! You know what

I'm talking about. And if you don't, you surely don't know what you're missing. Those simple pre-Pinterest parties were the best! Oh, she made sure everything matched the theme, though—napkins, plates, cups all in color coordinating fashion.

It was fascinating to me as a child, blue, yellow, then red solo cups stacked, alongside color coordinated napkins and plates. I'd never seen that anywhere, everything just matched so well. She even took the color scheme or theme in some way, shape, or form into the bathroom! So I guess in hindsight I had a very solid foundation on how to organize a party.

Thanks ladies, and my friends, thank you as well!

Into my teens and twenties I got promoted from pizza passer to MC. Since my mother and sister are both introverts, of course I'm the one that will run the verbal show, to this day! When there's an announcement to be made or a participation game to be played, I am the gal you ask. And not to mention, if you need a connection for full scale catering to a tray of cookies, I've got a person for that, too. Give them my name, they will give you a good price for sure. So much so that I'm the first choice when it comes to planning just about anything.

I actually don't mind it, I kind of like it. Orchestrating games, contests and conversation. I've got you covered, girl. That smaller, more intricate stuff, I have no problem delegating that away! And the kitchen, I try to stay out of that as much as I can. I prefer to purchase! Hey, you can't be good at everything and I sure know my limits with the things I enjoy and the things I do not.

So yes, growing up, I loved being the one making everyone

pay attention to the party girl as long as it was not me. I didn't (and still don't really) enjoy the spotlight, believe that or not.

Surprises, Good and Bad

I rarely celebrated my birthday with the exception of a surprise party for my 30th thrown for me by my sister, Tara, and my ex-husband. The surprise was fun I guess, but we had just received another surprise around that time, too. My father was diagnosed with stage IV lung cancer. He was only 48 and given a year and a half to live. I tried to be happy at the party, but my heart wasn't fully in it. I couldn't stop thinking about my dad, what would happen to my mom, and just how quickly things can change.

At the time of his diagnosis, the Billy Joel song, "Only the Good Die Young" played through my head on continuous loop. As cliché as it sounds, this truly was the case with my dad. He was such a good man. His diagnosis just didn't seem right or fair.

I wasn't the only one who felt this way about my dad. My dad was my mom's world. And everyone who knew him loved him. One of the few things I remember about my Great Aunt Pat, besides her always giving us a pack of that 25-cent yellow juicy fruit gum, was her saying, "You know your father. I have never met anyone that had anything bad to say about your father and I've been around a long time."

It was so true. He always had such a great disposition, even while working 3 jobs and being a volunteer fireman. He worked hard and lived a full life, even with what little he had living paycheck to paycheck, day by day.

Boy, he certainly enjoyed Sunday BBQ's, dart night, and time at the firehouse (both after working a long day, of course). He volunteered as a fireman I think for the camaraderie, to help people, and of course, for the shenanigans. He loved it, even ran for different positions, and eventually made it up to Captain in 2002. He was so proud.

So this surprise 30th birthday came at a pretty sad time in 2009. I really wanted to be in the moment, dance the night away, but the air seemed filled with this heavy weight, and it was hard to pretend to be happy, as you can imagine.

My father fought, but in 2011, he passed. And his passing, sad as it was, taught me something about the way we live. He had so many people that just adored him, and they surrounded us with that love, too. The Wanamassa Fire Department was so unbelievable to my family. They were at each service, with all the trucks, dressed in uniforms, feeding us, taking care of the repast. And I'll always be grateful for all the annual dinner dances we enjoyed together. My father had so many crazy dance moves; my mother absolutely was not a dancer. But gosh, how much they loved each other. They beat the odds as a couple, I have to say, that's for sure.

To honor my dad, my sister Tara and I signed up to become ladies auxiliary members at The Wanamassa Fire Department shortly after his passing. The ladies auxiliary supports the fire department in many ways. For example, if there is a fire, the ladies auxiliary comes with beverages and food to keep the firefighters hydrated and energized to fight the fire. Thankfully, in our small town, I've only had to do that once. The ladies auxiliary also fundraises to support the fire department. We find a lot of meaning doing this together, even after all these years, and much love and support as well. I highly suggest carrying on your family's legacy in some small way, joining a group or club, and surrounding yourself with a community of people who can be with you through life. As much as we all work to provide for our families, we all need to take time for BBQ's and enjoy life, like my dad taught us.

So how does all this relate to me celebrating my birthday and beginning this fun tradition? I guess I always found birthdays to be disappointing as I got older. I usually found myself a little let down on my birthday. I didn't have friends around me dancing or celebrating. It was just another night of the week, another day on the calendar.

A Sudden Shift and a Kickline

About two years after my dad passed, my dear friend Veera said to me, "Jess, how you spend your birthday is how your year will go." And that really made me think.

If that's the case, then boy I'm screwed.

Celebrating my birthday seemed frivolous. I had no disposable money. I was raising four children on my own. My ex had nothing to give us and I had nothing in the bank to fall back on. But I trusted Veera's advice. She's the type of woman who seemed to manifest her heart's desires, and I wanted in on that action. And I remembered my father having so much love around him even after he passed—how you live is how you die. Not sure I was really celebrating this life to the fullest, you know?

So, in 2014, I jumped into planning and I threw myself a party, simple as it was.

I picked a random weekday night because I didn't want to intrude on someone's weekend plans, and I figured the location wouldn't be as packed. This is still one of my birthday party rules: Weeknight Only! I literally invited hundreds of women via Facebook or text (for those non-Facebook using friends!), and then I just let it go. I didn't ask for an RSVP. I wanted this to be "a no-pressure, show up if you can, and let's celebrate casually together" kind of night. And boy oh boy, it was!

We went to Ninth Avenue Pier in a beachside town, near my home in New Jersey, Belmar. My friend Lesly, my sister Tara, and I grabbed dinner. While on the pier, we caught a magnificent sunset. The fun part was that throughout the night, dozens of friends strolled in and out! Each one who came in was a happy surprise. And all the while we were laughing, smiling, connecting with one another. We were even fortunate enough to enjoy a live band and an Elvis impersonator on the pier!! Totally unplanned but perfect. Talk about a blast!! Can you say, "Rockette Line to Frank Sinatra's New York, New York?" I didn't know I could kick so high anymore! We danced and socialized and in my heart I knew it was going to be the best year yet.

So this started the tradition. And since then, the party

brings me such joy. Whoever can make it, makes it. I follow the same simple formula:

Pick a week night.

Pick a fun, new venue.

Send an invite.

Let it go.

Show up and have a blast.

My philosophy is that we all work so hard (whether it be at home with our kids or as entrepreneurs, or in our jobs), we should spend more time enjoying life, connecting with friends new and old, simply celebrating. And, heck, if my parties give my friends and me a reason to be surrounded by love and support for a few hours, then so be it!

Finding My Ladies

So how did I find all these marvelous women that I get to call my friends? We are kind of a mixed bag, I guess you could say! A handful of them are my lifelong supporters a.k.a. friendship survivors of the middle school years, and the rest I guess I've picked up along the way. Through my twenties and thirties I made friends at various jobs including a life-changing job at the church. Then there was this women's networking group that my dear friend Una kindly invited me to called WIP, which stood for Women in Power. Other women from church went to WIP, but Una (with her stunning blue eyes and soft heart) was the only one who thought to include me.

Talk about a game changer!

Here I was a guest at their monthly meeting, just completely blown away by the caliber of these women. I had never been to anything like it! These women were doing all types of things. They had strong opinions; they were outspoken, yet kind. I was immediately intimidated. I was just working at the church in the after-school program, selling candles at night, and these women were doing business, some even owned their own businesses, and making things happen for real. They each had their own voice—strong ones. I wanted to hide in the corner, I felt I didn't belong there. They were all so incredible. And who was I? The unplanned girl who didn't have a pot to piss in.

Oh how unworthy we can make ourselves feel for no real reason at all. Una brought me there for a reason, and she believed I belonged even when I didn't. I guess she was right! All these years later and these strong WIP women are some of my best friends, celebrating my birthday right beside me.

How and why did I get so lucky? They love me, and they express it in so many ways, that at times I can be a bit overwhelmed. I don't come from an emotionally expressive family. God forbid my mother say those 3 little words. After a while I convinced myself I didn't need to hear them, and over time I've come to understand my mother's lack of mushy-ness much better.

I now know my mom loves me the best way she can. She isn't an emotional person, but growing up, she showed her love to me by teaching me what she thought was best for me, saying things like, "Work hard" or "Get a 9 to 5." To her, steady work was the only way to make ends meet, and I finally realized by her saying that, she was actually saying her version of "I love you." Because those 3 words hardly ever passed her lips, rarely at best. A steady job working hard for someone else might have been something my mom wanted for me, but I'd been working hard and paying bills for as long as I can remember, and still struggling to make ends meet. So boy oh boy, I just did not want this to be my story.

Being a part of WIP and maintaining friendships with powerful women who showed up for me in the most supportive ways helped me change my story.

I remember so clearly after each meeting, some of the ladies would go out for a drink to extend the night. I was new to the group so wasn't usually included in that part. But there was one time, after the meeting that I got the invite. This time it was to attend Natalie's birthday party at a fancy lounge called Watermark. First off, Natalie was a woman I was both drawn to and feared. I admired her but was absolutely intimidated by her. I couldn't have been more excited and nervous all at the same time. I was "in the group" finally, so here I was invited and to Natalie's birthday no less! And, yes, she is still one of my very best friends to this day.

You see, it just took one invitation from a stranger to change things forever for me. I imagine that is where my impulse to 'invite the world' to my parties comes from. What if Natalie never casually invited me to her birthday? It was something she didn't even think was a big deal, but oh boy, how it made such a difference for me.

Include everyone, people! You never know how it can

change them. And celebrate your birthday each and every year, not just "the big ones."

I really had no business throwing that first party or starting this tradition, but I did it anyway and it's proven to be one of the highlights of my year! Not just for me, but for many others too.

Make It Your Business to Celebrate

How will you celebrate your birthday? You can follow my simple formula to keep the energy high and the pressure low. Let's do this, girl! I dare you!

Pick the Date

So as I mentioned, week nights work best. First, weekends are tougher for many people. You aren't competing with family parties, getaways, or other plans. Second, places aren't as packed, leaving plenty of room for you and your friends to enjoy without feeling like stuffed sardines. So pick a week night right around your actual birthday.

Pick the Venue

Try to find venues that are unique and casual and don't require your friends to spend a lot. You don't want to pick that 5-Star restaurant that's $200 a plate no matter how much you've been dying to try it. Save that for date night, you don't want to alienate people based on budget! I like rooftop bars with no minimum (I don't even drink alcohol by the way), beachside open-air spaces because my birthday is in the summer, and we live right by the beach! I don't ever choose the sit-down restaurants that require everyone to sit at the same time, order, and eat. I find places that might serve apps at max. I like the idea of people popping in and out any time, and they can choose whether they want to spend money or not! Location is key so pick it wisely.

Send an Invite

Okay, here's the fun part! Because I keep the date during the week and the venue casual, my birthday becomes a time for me to gather old friends and new, my closest girls and people I'd like to know better, women with the best energy ever and those that need a boost. It isn't about a small tight circle (although I do love nights like that too).

My birthday celebration is a night for me to say thank you to those who stood by me and make new connections for the year ahead! So I invite everyone I like, respect, and admire who has good energy. I also invite some women who I believe could just use an invite or are desperately seeking something (they may need a dose of good vibes, you know?). In any given year, I send out hundreds of invites—how cool to see who shows up!!

So send out those invites to all kinds of friends you'd like to connect with. Make a Facebook Event but don't forget your friends who aren't on social media. They count too!!

No Regrets, Please

Often you see on invites "Regrets Only, Please." Well I have an opposite rule. Sure, you can tell me if you are coming, but I don't want to know if you CAN'T make it. What a buzzkill!

I understand if you are making food or reservations or need a headcount for a caterer—you need exact numbers. But let's be real, when people call and text before an event and tell you they cannot come, it stinks! So I make my parties not dependent on reservations or headcounts, hence the rule: don't call or text me if you can't make it, just don't show up. It's all good. Things come up and I still love you. I suggest you do the same, keep the energy good and your focus on all the people who do come!

Now, that's not to say I don't see patterns. So, watch out for my three-strike rule. What's that you say? If I invite you to my parties and you don't show up three times, I simply strike you from the list. Look, it's a total downer and I can take a hint if you don't want to come! So, I suggest you implement the same rule. No regrets, please!

See, isn't it awesome to make celebrating your business? I'll want an invite when you set up your next birthday celebration.

P.S. Exceptions apply to this formula, like on a milestone birthday! It's my 40th this year and you better believe I'm going big with a prom style bash, invite, rsvp, and all!!

CHAPTER

Two

A Crown of Daisies and a Whole Lot of Faith

"Faith is to believe what you do not see; the reward of this faith is to see what you believe."
~ Saint Augustine

I, Jessica Faith Varian, came into the world by way of c-section on August 26,1979. My parents, Mary and Tim Varian of Wanamassa (a little tiny section of Ocean Township, New Jersey), were two young fools in love. And when I say young, I mean young. My mother was just sixteen at the time of my birth, my father barely nineteen. They met two years prior—babies themselves, really, but inseparable at that.

The odds were against my parents, stacked high that this would not work out. My maternal grandmother, being very religious, wanted them to have a traditional church wedding. The church did not allow that, though. They were too young and pregnancy before marriage was a big no-no. Even for an "out of church" wedding, my grandparents had to grant them permission, which they did. My parents were so young, but still, I think anyone who knew them as a couple, knew their love was real. My grandparents had faith it would work out just fine, although it was really hard for them.

Two Young Hippies in Love

During a blizzard at my Great Aunt Pat's home at 1212 River Rd. in Belmar, New Jersey, in her knotty pine room, my parents exchanged their wedding vows. If you could see the photos, the vibe was totally hippy. My mother wore a light blue gunny sack and lace dress, a crown of daisies, and half a dozen small braids around her head with ballet slippers on her feet. After the wedding my mother rolled up the dress in a ball and donated it to the Salvation Army. Not surprising to me, that's my mother.

And then, just a few months after the wedding, I was ready to come into the world.

I was sitting on my mother's spine, making labor really difficult, so they did a c-section to deliver me. I guess I was always destined to find a way through pretty much any problem, hard as it may seem. I came out kicking and screaming with lungs of steel no less.

The Power in Our Names

They named me Jessica Faith, and all the family came

to see me in the hospital. The family still surrounds me for everything—Sunday dinners, week night get-togethers, birthdays, celebrations, good times and bad. I was never not meant to be in their eyes, and so they never treated me that way. I knew nothing of this growing up, just a regular little girl in a regular struggling to make ends meet family who just always knew by the grace of God it would all work out.

I was blessed by that middle name, let me tell you.

Faith (noun): complete trust or confidence in someone or something.

Talk about the PERFECT choice of middle name for me. Who knew my middle name would turn into something that has taken me through life in the ups and downs?

I didn't get the signifi cance as a child, at least not that I can remember. But my mother and father absolutely 100% believed that their faith would make everything okay—teen pregnancies were not so common back then, but they weren't worried. They had faith that I would be healthy, happy, and wonderful. And even though my parents came from different religious backgrounds—my mother a Roman Catholic whose family regularly attended mass and my father's family Methodist didn't attend church—they were two young people in love who believed in God, and that everything would work out the way it should. So because of their faith, they spoke life into mine and declared it so in my name. Funny thing is, I'm not sure they even thought so deeply about it or could know the impact that middle name would have on my life. But oh boy, it did.

Now as for my first name, definitely not so deep. They

named me Jessica thanks to the Allman Brothers' song (gotta love the 70's!). Wouldn't change it for the world. I do love me some Allman Brothers. This might give you another clue about my parents, they had faith, but they also enjoyed the hippy life style.

And unconventional as it was, my upbringing, the unconditional love by my big family has made me who I am today, with roots I never want to forget. That's why I still use my maiden name, Varian.

There is so much meaning in the names we choose, the names we are given, and the names we hold on to. My mother spoke life into my calling, by giving me the middle name Faith. How powerful words can be.

I pretty much live my life with unwavering faith that everything will be okay and work out. Growing up, it was kind of our family's motto. We just knew it would be all right, somehow, some way, even if it was pretty frustrating at times.

The fact that "everything was going to be okay" was so ingrained in us, that it was just the norm. Then as I got older I very much believed this and that turned into me having "faith" that everything will work out. What a powerful name I was given that has continued to help me in the tougher moments of life.

One quote I love so dearly is from the Marigold Hotel movie, "Everything will be okay in the end because if it's not okay it's not the end."

True.

So very true.

To remind myself of this (because heck I am human and we all have bad days), I have two signs on my wall, "Have Faith" and "Let your Faith be bigger than your fear." I say Amen to that—although sometimes easier said than done because it really is a lifelong lesson.

Some people find it odd how I seem to stay so calm in situations others would be completely crazed over. I just know everything will work out just as it should when the time is right. And that knowing comes from my faith. When I think about it, faith is just really a choice. You can choose to have it or not. But if I chose NOT to have it, man my life would be one big fear-fest, I'd be curled up in a fetal position never leaving the house. So, no thank you. I will take faith over fear any day.

Maybe This is Where I Get It . . .

My mother was always considered wise beyond her years. Maybe being the youngest of four brothers had something to do with that? Oh yes, she was very nurturing, loved taking care of the kids she would babysit for, and just seemed more mature than most of her peers. My mom never cared about the typical things that girls her age would. She always stayed in her own path, didn't worry about being popular and all the other things teens can get so wrapped in. She always remained true to her own self with no apologies.

So my mother never thought for one second of any other option than simply having me. According to her family and friends she never questioned her decision one bit, even though she was still a child herself. She was completely confident. I've been told by many people that my parents never doubted their story. With faith, they would figure life out together.

Before you knew it my Irish twin brother Tim was born, then 2 years later, my sister Tara came into the world blessing my parents with 3 perfect cherubs (of course) under the age of 4. You bet being the oldest sibling came with lots of responsibility, even at that young age. Oh boy, I remember when my maternal grandfather would come home (did I mention we all lived together?) he would bring us a bag of plain m&m's for me to split 3 ways. Try dishing out 100 m&m's and making it an even split at 5 years old. Okay, maybe sometimes it would be two for me, one for you, but luckily my siblings were so young they didn't even notice! Maybe that explains my love of order and chocolate? Hmm. I wonder.

And oh so many times, I would have to be the brave one. Me, little old me, Jessica Faith braving the creepy noises to find out what we heard and calm my siblings down. I was the oldest, so I had to suck it up, walk in the dark room, and see what freaked us all out. I took on the role of the protector, the sorter, the teacher, the organizer, the tie-breaker, the fight stopper, the responsible one. All that being said, the pros far outweighed the cons. I'm so lucky to have them as siblings because they now go along with all of my crazy shenanigans, even though sometimes it's outside their comfort zone. We are quite the opposites in some ways.

My parents did whatever it took to keep us afloat, and they did the best they could the only way they knew how—working hard and having faith. My dad pumped gas during the day when we were really young, and on occasion kind people would give him a tip, and any tip money he got went to eating lunch. Then he would head over to a private school in the evening to do janitorial duties; working late into the evening cleaning stuff the kids left behind, sanitizing the bathrooms, and more just to make ends meet. Later in life, my dad stopped working at the gas station and school to become a mechanic which he did at a few places every week. He always worked several jobs at once let me tell you.

My mother would work the late shift at the convalescent center so they could save on child care. She was home during the day. Dad worked his 3 jobs, and when he got home she left to do her shift. Looking back I wonder how on earth they had the energy to do anything. And this cycle never really stopped. For years and years my dad worked all 3 jobs and even was a volunteer fireman. As we got older my mom worked at the hospital as an emergency tech in the emergency room. When we were lucky she would bring us one of the 15 cent candies home with her from the gift shop, which she would charge to her employee account as a treat for us. Boy did I love the pastel Mentos the most!

So considering all the facts, looking back, my parents made it despite their many challenges. They were the fortunate ones. They loved and cherished each other through the ups and downs of their 32-year marriage and 34 years of being together. Their time was cut far too short, no doubt about that. After my dad's diagnosis, before he passed, they did get to renew their vows on their 30th wedding anniversary in our family church Holy Spirit in Asbury Park with friends, family, children and grandchildren in attendance. Having so many ups and downs with my own love life, watching them renew their vows renewed my faith in all that is good.

Strong as my mother is, I know she suffers from broken heart syndrome. There is no doubt about that. She doesn't easily show it, but I know she misses my dad so much every single day. But wouldn't you, after all of those years of that person being your one and only? It does make me question sometimes if love is really worth it—I mean seeing her suffer that way so badly. Her pain turns physical for her often. It's heart wrenching to watch and see. But truly, if I could have just an ounce of that kind of love, through and through, maybe I would just risk the broken heart and allow myself to fall madly in love with someone. She does have a broken heart, but she also has faith that they will meet again. I have faith so strong today, because of the faith they had in bringing our family into the world.

A Miracle Here and There

So now you have a glimpse into my parents' love, my appointed name, and how faith really can move mountains, feed families, and get you through. But while my parents had so much faith, I saw them work so very hard and struggle so very much. I think faith does make all things possible, but shouldn't life be just a little easier than all this work? Sure they had their share of gatherings, celebrations, and joy-filled moments, and all in all they felt blessed and happy. For some reason, I wanted to propel their faith and honor their teachings in an even bigger way. Deep down I felt destined to be "Jessica Faith," the name I was given to be a person full of faith and determined to go farther. And that faith I had brought me so many miracles. Miracles in ways big and small, miracles in moments where all the faith I had would just shift whatever current situation I was in with the blink of an eye or in one deep breath. I am always amazed at how that happens.

And let me tell you, I've experienced my share of miraculous situations. Whether it be from a Good Samaritan paying my bills after my water was shut off, or getting into the perfect townhouse at the perfect time for just the right amount of time, or finding a home right by the water (what a dream come true), or a kind stranger leaving me a check for thousands of dollars at my door with Reilly's birthday and Christmas both right around the corner, no joke!!

I only hope I have been a helper, a source of a miracle to someone as so many have been to me. I think you have to be in many ways just as open to giving as you are to receiving, if not giving even more so. Faith is the thread between the two. You have to have faith that when you give something, you are being a blessing to someone and you're not going to suffer too much by the giving. I learned this firsthand from my mother, and still sometimes I wonder how she does it. So often when she had few resources herself but would see another struggling person, she would give them whatever little she had to offer—a ride, a meal, a cigarette, a few dollars. She had faith it would work out. And still does! And so I do my best to do the same, giving whatever I can to the church, donation centers, families in need.

And I think it's reciprocal, what goes around comes around, and when you need that miracle, you better believe it just might happen for you too.

And of course, even if there's no miracle, and I have a bit of discomfort, pain, suffering, the only way I can get through those times is by faith. Trusting there is a bigger plan than my own, and it will all work out. Maybe it is the blessing in disguise. I try and think that I have done (most of the time) right by my parents. I've tried to make them proud that I am doing the very best as often as I can, and that I am living up to that big, divinely appointed middle name. I always look for the silver lining, look for the blessing, seek the rainbow in the rain because it might turn out to be one of life's greatest joys!

Make It Your Business to Have a Little Faith

Look for Signs Everywhere

Faith isn't something that you are on your own with, although it may feel like that sometimes. There are cues everywhere, in everything. Look for signs along the way and when you can't see them just ask God or the Universe to show them to you! One time I even asked the Universe to have a bird poop on me if I was doing the right thing, and guess what? The next day, it happened!

Use Your Words for Good

Words are very powerful and can literally speak faith into any situation. Just like my middle name is a constant reminder to have faith, use and choose your words for good. When you speak with doubt or uncertainty, your whole energy level changes! Speak with faith and you will feel more faithful. It really is that simple!!

Know By Heart Your Go-To Quotes

Having a family motto or a list of "go-to" quotes can help lift you up when times are tough! Make a list of these quotes and add to it any time you see or hear one that makes you feel more full of faith. Think of these quotes like affirmations and repeat them to yourself often. You will be amazed at how the quotes become your own personal mantra for having more faith.

Put the Faith-Filled Reminders in Plain Sight

Having pictures, wooden signs, even magnets or scrap pieces of paper with words or visuals that remind you of your faith is super helpful for subconsciously sending a message to yourself to stay in faith. We are all human and can have times where we start to waver, in those times look to your reminders!

CHAPTER
Three

Family Roots and Gaining Wings

"Generations pass like leaves fall from our family tree. Each season new life blossoms and grows benefiting from the strength and experience of those who went before."
~ The Talmud

G rowing up in our home on Grassmere Ave in Wanamassa had to be one of the greatest gifts my parents could have given us. Rather than get an apartment they could afford, my parents chose to live with my grandparents because my mother felt it was the best for us in many ways. They call Wanamassa "the Mayberry" of our larger town of Ocean Township, and I'm okay with that. We grew up running around the parks, catching turtles at the lakes, and staying out 'til the street lights came on. Wanamassa was (and still is) a true gem of a place to grow up in. Oh yeah, I loved my little Mayberry so much, that I couldn't wait until I was able to purchase my second home just a block away from my childhood home. I thought I was the luckiest girl alive to have my children live in Wanamassa and attend Ocean Township schools.

Was it the smartest decision I've ever made? Heck no! But sometimes we make foolish decisions so we can look back and learn from them. I was in a different place back then, and homes and I, well, let's just say I've had quite a few over the years. I will get into all of that a little later in the chapter. I think it's important to share how I ended up with this "dreamer", "go for it", "the world is yours" attitude and why I have grown into an abundance mindset, even before I knew really what that even meant.

Abundance vs. Nothing

So the opposite of abundance is nothing, right? People call it many things, nothing, lack, dead broke, scarcity. Well, I learned about that scarcity stuff in a roundabout way. And that's pretty much how we all learn, just by living, things get ingrained into you—some things are amazing and other things are the opposite of that, they suck.

Mine was a family of "make-ends-meeters." I knew my parents got paid on Fridays, so toward the end of the week, almost every week, they would have to borrow money from one of my relatives. My father was always in the automotive field, starting as the gas attendant and eventually moving his way up to a union master technician. My mother worked in a nursing home and then the emergency room of a local hospital. I had no idea how much they made until much later in life, but it was very apparent they never quite made enough. My parents didn't have credit cards (that I know of) that they could fall back on, as I do now. So I get it and know that I definitely would've had to borrow some money too, at certain times, and actually I have.

The cash in our home was tight for sure. I remember being a Girl Scout and even joining a youth group was tough for my parents to swing, but they found a way. Girl Scout dues at that time may have been $25 or so for the year, but for one reason or another my parents couldn't give the full $25 in just one payment. Luckily the troop leader let them spread out some payments over time. I thought nothing of it, other than as a Girl Scout we had to keep track of attendance and dues. I can't even imagine what that might have been like as a parent. I have known struggles believe me but not to that extent, I suppose.

I was very close to my grandmother, and I remember on occasion she would hand my mom a $20 bill. Oh it was such a treat because mom would get us Carvel. I think that is why I struggle sometimes raising my own children. In my childhood, nothing was taken for granted or expected. Carvel was a big deal, not something that was just given to us regularly. The ice cream was special. I know times have changed, and maybe I've raised my children differently, but they definitely don't consider an ice cream cone a big deal. Now having their own bedrooms, that would be the bee's knees, especially for the boys!

Perspective is funny though. I have many people who have told me they need a 3-bedroom home, but they only have one or two kids!! Say what?! There were times we packed into a two bedroom for five of us. So I can't say my kids are completely spoiled, but they've witnessed my evolution and they no longer have a mom who believes in lack or scarcity. Sometimes that can bite me in the butt, and I do want them to value even the smallest of things, as I do. I'm trying to be a good example for them with finances. I'm trying to talk the talk and walk the walk.

Growing up, my parents weren't the strongest financial role models and I don't believe in all honesty their parents were either. I mean I believe they all did the best they could, and maybe even they just did as they had seen from their parents. It's kind of like passed down generations of living in lack with a scarcity mindset. Who was our family to be abundant? My mother's famous words to us as we got older were, "Get a 9-5 and save your money!" I never understood the 'saving money' part. They did not save a dime! They said they couldn't but looking back, I do believe it's a mindset. They thought they couldn't, so they didn't. Boy did it take me years to understand that one. Our money mindset determines our wealth, no matter what you have in the bank or how big your house is after all.

There were never talks of college and maybe that's because my parents both got their GED, and their parents never went to college so it's just a topic they did not know about. When my oldest son became a senior in high school, I was relentless in asking for help from the high school guidance counselor because I did not know a thing. I'm happy to report Jared is the first of my direct family to attend Brookdale Community College, where he is learning the ropes! I am proud of him breaking that generational thing. We are not stuck by the past, but we grow by our roots. They make us stronger, but they should not define us or limit us. I am not saying you need to go to college, but it should never be something you think you are unworthy of, no way! And if you want to go, girl you better go for it, no matter what your age, too. College or any life goals don't just happen. I mean, in high school I think I applied to Monmouth University, I had no idea if I did it right and I don't think I ever even heard back from them. My friends had applied to colleges, but I really had no idea what was going on. I guess I assumed it just happened, you didn't really have to go after it. Now I know that whatever we want, we must pursue fiercely.

Sex, Sins, and Words Unspoken

Let's talk about sex, wait let's not. You know that catchy song by Salt and Pepa in the 90's. So in my home and growing up, sex wasn't discussed like at all, and I was perfectly fine with that. I think it was an Irish Catholic thing, but I'm not sure. The only time I do remember is my mother calling me to her room on the top floor of the house, on a totally random weeknight. She said, "Jessica, do you know about sex, you know like they teach you in school?"

Oh boy. I was beet red and totally not ready to talk to my

mother about this one. So of course I was like, "Yes." And quickly tried to end that talk.

I believe she asked me one more simple basic question and I knew the answer, I think it had something to do with sperm. Then by God's good grace, my uncle was walking up the stairs obviously ending the awkward conversation never to be spoken about again.

I worked at a 5 & 10 during high school and after. I met this cute guy with nice eyes, and life seemed just lovely. But then suddenly, every morning while opening the store, I began getting so sick, like running to the toilet in our damp, dark, dank tiny store bathroom to throw up. I was just nineteen, and thought, "Wow, why am I getting sick like this?"

At one point I told my mother I was throwing up every morning at work. Believe me when I tell you it never occurred to me that I could be pregnant. Honestly, naive, so much so, that one day my parents took me to the hospital for this "mysterious illness" that happened every morning. Within minutes of being seen, a nurse asked if I could be pregnant, in front of my parents no less!

Who me?

Wide-eyed, in total denial, I was in disbelief. But really, could it be? Well let's just say it wasn't a crazy flu of some sort. I was in fact pregnant with full on stereotypical morning sickness, and with a baby due on 12/24/98.

My parents seemed fine and accepting of the fact, I mean they were young in love once too, right? I feel a little bit like I repeated the pattern, young and pregnant. In the Catholic

Church that is a sin after all, but my parents never made me feel like that. Well, my dad might have been a little upset, but my mother certain didn't let him say anything otherwise. She was kind of like that a lot. Considering I would be making her a grandmother at the wise old age of 35!!

35 people! I'm older than that now, and I couldn't fathom being a grandmother, and knowing how challenging it would be for any of my children. I share with them now, 27 is a good minimum age to start a family.

So I had my son Jared, and the cute guy never turned into my husband. As a young, single mom, I had a lot of growing up to do and fast. Eventually I met another cute guy, we fell in love, had more babies, and got engaged. Although I like things in order in my home, I was never one to feel the need to do things in order with my personal life. I am a romantic, hopeless, always learning. I wanted to get on with this happily married couple with the white picket fence life that I always dreamed of, so I decided when Pat and I got engaged, it was time.

Dream Homes and Nightmares

When my fiancé and I went to buy our first home in 2003, my parents offered to give us five thousand dollars to help, but there was a stipulation. We had to stay within 5 miles of them, no getting out of dodge if we wanted that money. Well we needed the money, and I didn't want to go that far anyway.

We looked in several towns. Wanamassa was out of the question on our very small pre- approval rate, but we were blessed to find a nice home in Neptune, a town right next door. My mother would drop off a box of munchkins every Sunday after she went to the 8 am mass at Holy Spirit. The kids loved it and my parents were happy. So my parents instilling in us again, family stays close and family first. We lived in Neptune for almost 3 years, and when Reilly was born, the 700-square foot house was no longer going to do for the 5 of us. And soon thereafter with Damian on the way, I thought we definitely needed more space. Plus the dreamer in me wanted the kids in the Wanamassa school system just like my mother.

It was 2006 and the mortgage business was booming. You didn't need too much paperwork to get a mortgage, and since we thought we could actually afford to move, we were completely sold on the idea. And so we bought our second home, moved the family in, and were back in Mayberry. It was a dream come true for a little while before it turned into a total nightmare.

Did me or my ex-husband think through how we would actually pay for the mortgage we were approved for? It was double our first mortgage amount. Um. That would be a no. Did we have money in the bank for emergency repairs or kid stuff or any of the typical things that come up? Again, no. We were in la la land, playing house and living in the town I grew up in. We stretched and struggled to make ends meet for a little while. Finally my ex-husband just decided it was too much stress, after cashing in the tiny 401k I was so proud of, and selling everything we could, it was pretty much over—we just couldn't pay the mortgage.

You heard me. We couldn't pay the mortgage. We couldn't honestly afford the house we got approved for, and we were in the shits. Our marriage was crumbling, our house was being foreclosed on, and there were nights I just couldn't breathe because I was so worried I would wake up the next day with a padlock on the door. I had to leave and take the kids with me. And so I moved into a rental on Garven in the same town.

Oh, that home was filled with many ups and downs. We had lots of celebrations, big ones, including my ladies only Christmas ornament party, to littles ones, like celebrating birthdays, having the girls over to make vision boards, and just fun get togethers—those were some good times. But I had low times there, too, like when the water was turned off because my ex-husband decided not to pay child support. He actually picked up the kids, had them shower at our old home, then dropped them back to me. I relied on him too much financially, even though he proved himself unreliable. And this up and down relationship continued until one day a good Samaritan (and also a client) left me an envelope of hope with money to pay my bills.

Then I decided to begin my independence from my ex, I had to learn the system of applying for state health care, food stamps, utilities assistance. I swear if you have never had the good fortune of going through it, it's seriously a full-time job. Don't get me started on the paperwork. But it's what a mother does to do whatever she can to support and take care of her children. And it gave us a start on our own. Yes, there were times the water got shut off in our rental and I had to take the kids to the other house just to bathe them. It was a real peach of a time, let me tell you. I could not see a way out of it all.

We lived on Garven for a while, but even with state assistance, I could not keep up with the $1650 rent solely, so it was back to my mother's with the kids. It wasn't ideal, and not a permanent situation, I just needed to figure some stuff out. I was a single, sole support mother of 4, trying to start a business, and working for the church. Not to mention, I was also a Girl Scout leader, a volunteer, and dating a new guy. Time and funds were stretched to the max.

In my personal life, after the divorce was finalized and I started dating again, I got serious with a guy (another charmer—see a pattern here?). I wanted desperately to be on our own again, and so of course I always had feelers out there for a new home.

After hearing through the grapevine of a friend of a friend whose home was going to be on the market for rent in Tinton Falls, I went to take a look! It was huge. The vaulted ceilings, open floor plan, fireplace, and don't get me started on the master bedroom and bathroom. The gentleman who owned it wanted to feel like he was on vacation every day of his life. Imagine going from living with your parents to a serene, gorgeous getaway style home? Oh boy, I could. And so I just jumped on it, with my boyfriend so it would be affordable, and voila! It was official, we were moving, and the kids were changing schools.

For my oldest, Jared, it would now be his 3rd school district, and he was only in 7th grade. For him, I always thought of it as a blessing, because he adapted so quickly, made friends so easily, and to this day I still call him the mayor. He knows people from all over and brings them together for a pickup game of basketball. What a beautiful quality.

So we were in!

I believed in my heart we were settling down as a family once and for all, and I made a promise to myself that our utilities would never be shut off again.

At that time I was living with the boyfriend and we had a financial agreement that he rarely made good on and especially on time. Things were going downhill but I felt stuck, mainly due to finances and that part he wasn't even consistent on. After speaking with my dear friend Terri I realized that it was a form of abuse and she suggested I go to speak to the people of 180 Turning Lives Around. Was she crazy, how was that abuse? I was so mind boggled at the time, but the situation didn't improve. I felt trapped, so I called and made an appointment to see what it was all about. During my first of 5 complimentary sessions I learned that there were 8 different forms of abuse, and here I only thought of the physical kind.

How could it be I was a victim of domestic abuse, in several areas of their pie chart?

I continued to go speak to the counselor where she suggested options, gave me gift cards for food and most importantly just listened. I'm not saying my ex-boyfriend was a bad person; he was human, he had his issues, and then he brought them home to me.

Although I knew I was tolerating abuse, I stayed. I didn't

have the internal strength at that time to just up and leave. I prayed for a way out, though. I knew in my heart this was not how it should be. My family deserved stability, and this was anything but stable. So the godsend came when my landlord called and needed to put the house on the market and needed us out in less than a month. When this occurred, I knew it was an answer to my prayer.

Knowing this also made me realize I was strong enough, and I truly believed that I could make it work alone somehow even in these crazy high-rent New Jersey shore towns. I finally had the talk with him and made it known he would not be coming with us. Although I felt badly, I also felt positive this was the right thing to do.

And then another door opened.

I've never been one to be shy about my challenges. I put the word out that we were looking for a rental. My dear friend Krista heard her old rental was on the market for rent again. Krista made the connecting text and next thing you know we were moving to West Long Branch. The rent was even $400 higher than the rent I was sharing with my ex-boyfriend, but I knew I would make it somehow someway. It was a stretch for sure, but we lived in that beautiful townhome for 4 years. There was just 1 month that I didn't have enough to make the rent, but a dear friend came to me, gave me the difference, and just asked that I work it off by organizing her home. She believed in me and still believes in me even when I don't see it.

My friends, my dear friends are everything. Through all my extraordinary hardship, exciting times, tragic times, highs and lows they have been there. There is more than a handful I trust with my life and my children's lives. They have listened, supported, encouraged, and just loved me. As you can imagine, I have had my fair share of challenges as a single, sole provider for 4 children and CEO of my company. Oh boy, the obstacles I have faced. I have never really done it alone.

Making Moves, Breaking Molds, and Understanding More

I have to laugh thinking about all of the homes we've lived in. My kids sure are resilient, I tell you, even if they don't appreciate the ice cream from time to time. They are flexible, that is for sure. We have lived in every size and shape home imaginable. Well I never lived in a mansion at least not yet, but you get the idea. From our little place in Wanamassa where Reilly and Damian shared a bedroom and Noah and Jared took the other, to the 2 bedroom home where the boys had a bedroom in the unfinished basement with no heat to our 3-story townhome where we converted an office for Reilly's bedroom and used a shower curtain as a door! And in our current single-family ranch, all of the bedrooms do in fact have doors, but Noah and Damian still share a room.

I believe the size of the space is irrelevant. So I've spent more money to put our family in a good location, a structurally sound and well-maintained home where we could figure out the best use of the space. I also believe that sometimes you just have to leap, and the net appears. I mean, I had no business getting myself into higher rents on my own, but I had faith and worked my ass off, and did it anyway.

I know with absolute certainty that the ladies I surrounded myself with showed me that abundance is mine, I just had to be open to receiving and knowing I am worthy of it. I had to overwrite the scarcity programming from multiple generations of my family.

One of the results of this lack lifestyle is addiction, and I had grown up in a family with different levels of different kinds of addictions. Of course, my family is incredible, addictions didn't make them bad people. They are normal, everyday, hardworking human beings. Addictions are so common, and it happens all the time to many families. From gambling, drinking, smoking and getting high, but these addictions equaled scarcity and fear. And that's why abundance just seemed so unfamiliar but also oddly appealing.

Now listen, no one put anyone in jeopardy or danger during these times. But I did know, like really know, in middle school I didn't want to be like everyone else. I didn't want to do anything—no recreational drug use (which was so prevalent at the time), like marijuana, acid, and whatever else!! Actually I couldn't even tell you because it just was not and would never be an option for me. I was not interested, like not in the least! Drinking, no. Lose control and act different—I never understood it. Yes, I have had a drink or so throughout the years, but it was nothing I ever went and sought out. Plus I just couldn't fathom why people would spend so much money on a drink? I mean for that price I could get a milkshake, now that's what I'm talking about. Gambling thank goodness never caught my attention. So for many reasons, I felt like the black sheep of my big family. I mean my family is amazing, and we all have our things. Mine is chocolate and a daily soda, maybe two.

I think as I've gotten older, you know I am just turning forty, so I am kind of a full-fledged adult now, I realized that understanding my family roots allows me to honor them in our differences as opposed to feeling like a hero or a victim. I mean, as I said every family has their stuff, I'm sure one day my own kids will write about the things I did that they didn't agree with or understand! But if you think your parents and grandparents were wrong, then you make a change, you're like the hero. And if you don't make the change, you're like the victim with a "poor me look at how I grew up" mentality"my parents never taught me XYZ".

Umm, I don't think so. My family has taught me so much and gave me the foundation to break the mold. I would definitely not be the person I am today if I didn't have a strong, calm, cool, generous yet tough, rarely say I love you mother and a hardworking, helping others, life of the party yet stays on the sidelines father. I challenge you to look at your roots differently. It's so freeing when you are not trying to live up to perfection or being strapped down by circumstance.

Make It Your Business to Understand Your Family Roots and Reach for More

Understand Your Roots

Where you come from is so important. Whether you had a loving family or a cold one, whether you deem your upbringing blessed or a mess, there are so many things that you can learn about who you are, what you want, and what makes you uniquely you when you take time to understand your family roots.

Learn from Your Mistakes

Sometimes mistakes are just lessons that hurt like heck. Don't beat yourself up over the mistake, just try to learn the lesson! If you find yourself in the same situation over and over, realize you probably still have something you can learn. Life can be a mirror, don't be afraid to look at it!

Ask Ask Ask

Don't be afraid to ask people for help! Be vulnerable and put out there what you need, desire, or are looking for! And on the flip side, be willing to help others, too. I know so many blessings have come my way simply because I had the courage to ask people for help!

Break the Mold

It's totally fine to branch out from your family roots a bit! You don't have to be a carbon copy of your parents or siblings, you are your own person! Too often we limit ourselves and all our possibilities because we try to fit a mold formed by prior generations. Instead, reach for the stars, and be your own person!

Section 2

Finding Your Calling

"I had no business becoming an entrepreneur, I was always told to get a 9 to 5...but I discovered a path, took the leap, and did it anyway."

CHAPTER Four

A Sweet Taste of Entrepreneurship

"Someone is sitting in the shade today because someone planted a tree a long time ago."
~ Warren Buffet

I come from a long line of blue collar, hardworking, work for a boss, live paycheck to paycheck, make ends meet thanks be to God kind of people. My grandfather on my mom's side worked for the electric company and my grandmother worked retail on and off. My grandfather on my dad's side painted houses and his wife (my nanny) worked in a bank randomly when they needed extra money. My mom worked various jobs in the convalescent center, in the ER, helping the elderly, in retail, as did my dad who worked as a janitor, mechanic, gas station attendant, and picked up a retail job later in life to bring in extra income. Well, I think you get the picture.

He was always working.

My mother just wanted me to have something stable, and to her that meant getting a solid 9 to 5, maybe as a sales clerk or manager somewhere, working for somebody or in a store. But that's kind of where the guidance in that area ended.

I mean, growing up I had no idea what I wanted to be—my family didn't really discuss things like that. As any kid does, I started to just think of a job that would be fun for me. So when it came to 6th grade career day, I was torn between a veterinarian and a beautician. Back then I had no idea what that would actually entail as in schooling and things like that, they just both sounded fun to me. I went with beautician, and I wrote my essay, brought in a maroon blow-dryer (if I remember correctly, my family didn't use blow-dryers, so we borrowed one), and presented my project complete in a lab coat from the ER where my mom worked, holding up my poster board, and there you have it! Voila, Jessica the beautician. I'm not sure I thought of either of those professions after that day.

I really didn't have a clue growing up to as what women did for careers. I mean I knew my mom helped people in the nursing home and then at the hospital, and my maternal grandmother worked retail, but that was about all of the firsthand knowledge I had until I joined Girl Scouts in the third grade (when it was still cool to be in Girl Scouts). What an impact! I'm even Facebook friends still with 2 of my troop leaders, Mrs. Sherman and Mrs. Hart, who might I say are very proud of all that I have achieved so far. Wink wink.

It was during those meetings that I was exposed to things

I had never been taught before. We were responsible for dues, attendance, planning events, and I sure soaked up every minute of it. I still remember Mrs. Sherman's home on Vina Ave, built in the early 1900's. It used to be a rooming house for wealthy people during the speakeasy time, with all its nooks and crannies, oh what a neat place. I remember one day seeing a list on the fridge for an upcoming party she was having. She had a timeline of the weekend and when things should be done, detailed down to the minute, and a timeline that you worked backwards, pure genius. Totally blew me away. Guess it really stuck with me and came in handy because many years later I began to use that same system and still do.

Badges, Sashes, and Cookie Sales

Through Girl Scouts, I learned so many things. Oh, boy, we were exposed to lots of great stuff. I still remember one meeting, one of the leaders was selling Mary Kay at the time, and as practice, she gave us a demonstration on taking care of your face! Then there was the time I went to another leader's office in Red Bank and saw women in business in action. Wow, just wow. I felt like I was a million miles from home. And then there were the badges you could earn by doing a few activities and having an adult sign off for you. I was obsessed! I mean truly I would do whatever to earn them, then my grandmother would sign, and the badges would come in. I would be so proud. I even sewed them on my sash myself. I still have the badges and sash. Can you say goody-goody? Heck yeah I was.

Oh, and to top it off, I lived for the cookie sales. Yes, you heard me. I remember the first time I was introduced to the cookie order form sheet. I was in love. I knew I wanted to do my very best and fill up every single line of that long form. It was so cool! I had absolutely no qualms about asking my family, friends—whoever was in my life knew I was selling cookies. I canvased the whole neighborhood, too. I had no issue going door to door, because I thought this was so cool. We always had to set ourselves a goal. My first goal might have been 60 boxes. Well with all my efforts and of course my parents help as well, I was nearing the 100-box mark. When I hit that, I was so excited. Then when the cookies came in we had to sort them. For me, talk about a dream come true—organizing, then filling the orders, delivering the cookies, collecting the money. I was in my glory. The next year I hit 130, no one was stopping me!

I'm eternally grateful for those years, I feel forever indebted to the Girl Scouts, and of course my troop leaders. I didn't realize it at the time how pivotal those experiences would be in my later years. Girl Scouts made such an impact on me, that the moment I knew I was having a daughter in 2004, I tried to apply to be a leader! I wanted to get the ball rolling early you know. I sadly found out that I would have to wait at least 4 years to begin the process, but trust me when the time came, I was first in line to form a kindergarten troop. I was ready, I found a co-leader, my neighbor Terisa, who had a daughter Sarah the same age as my daughter Reilly. She was so excited to be a co-leader. Total score.

Terisa was a character, let me tell you. Where I was more reserved, she would let anything fly right out of her mouth. Mostly not in front of the girls, of course. Telling me stories of cutting school, hopping a fence in her Catholic school skirt…I was thinking, "how could you even do that?" I did a few off the wall things myself, but dare I ever admit to it. And with the girls, she was more of the jokester while I was the one making sure they got everything done. We definitely balanced each other out.

Running an Organized, Tight Ship

So from Reilly's kindergarten through 7th grade school years, I was a co-leader for her Girl Scout troop. We met often, we held the young girls accountable, taught them responsibility and the importance of teamwork, held them to high standards, and all in all brought in as many life skills as we could, as my troop leaders always did for me. For example, each girl would have a responsibility—one would take attendance, one would lead the Pledge of Allegiance, one would check the bathrooms before we left, one would sweep the floors, one set up the chairs. Yes, we ran a tight ship. And you bet we were not just your everyday "arts and crafts" troop. We did things, lots of big things from collecting food for the needy to visiting nursing homes to overnight outings to running a successful blood drive for their bronze award, and at the end of the year celebration, we got the whole family involved.

And, of course we did cookie sales, that was a must. We

asked the girls to make their goals and we worked backwards with their goal number to get their daily (see how handy that is). We raised the bar when the girls were just 6 and 7 years of age, to sell 1500 boxes of cookies—there were only 14 of them so that was a stretch for us, because the year before we sold just under a 1,000 I think. So raising the bar adding 50% more to that for these young girls was a lot. You know I love a big goal. But this was even more amazing than just a goal, this was to teach them that when they have a vision, work to reach the goal, the reward is even bigger!

Let me explain. This particular year Girls Scouts of America would be celebrating their 100-year anniversary by having a huge all-day affair at Liberty State park on the Hudson. Even more incredible, the evening would end with a concert by Sara Bareilles and fireworks. Her music was fun and inspiring, just the energy we wanted our troop to be around. So of course, my co-leader and I wanted all the girls to earn their tickets with cookie money. Our audacious 1500-box goal would do just that. The girls worked hard and guess what?! We did! The 100-year celebration was definitely something I will never forget.

There are so many memories that I made with those girls over the years. Goodness, I could write a whole book about it, and just might! I can only hope to have made an impact, even on just one of them, like my leaders did for me.

So I just went on a tangent a bit. I guess you can tell how much Girl Scouts changed my life. I mean, cookies sales gave me my first taste of business, and after that, I was hooked—

school fundraisers, bake sales, book fairs—you better watch out I was the girl to do it all! Heck yeah!

I mean of course we had your typical small-town corner lemonade stands, we always did quite well and more times than not we'd somehow acquire an animal, too. Like the time a complete stranger buying lemonade showed up with a shoebox holding a large guinea pig. He gave it to us as he casually said, "Keep the change." Surprisingly our parents were fine with it, as least for a while. Crazy as it sounds, I always felt people were generous and kind. And boy did I like making some decent cash for myself, especially since I was walking distance to Carvel, 7-11, the 5 & 10. You know I spent that money the minute I got it!

Make It Your Business to Find the Things that Spark the Light in You

Play Like a Child

Look back to what inspired you as a child. Try to remember all the games you liked to play, the activities you loved, the things that you did for pure fun. Often times the gifts we have shine through in the stuff we loved to do way back when! If you can't remember, ask your older relatives, look through old photo albums, play music that was popular during your childhood. Soon enough, the memories will come flooding back!

Give Yourself Permission to Enjoy Your Work

So often we put work in a boring box and think it has to be something we don't enjoy, or else it wouldn't be work. But nothing could be further from the truth. If something brings you joy, give yourself permission to incorporate that right into your job or even start a side hustle!

Set Goals and Work Hard

Having clear goals gives you something to work towards. Make them attainable but not easy. Make the goal a stretch for you, and don't give up! Use your creativity and resources to reach whatever goal you set, and once you hit the mark, set an even bigger one! Don't forget to reward yourself along the way!

CHAPTER
Five

Batteries, Tires, Bulbs, and a Brick House Breakdown

"In the end you should always do the right thing even if it's hard." ~ *Nicholas Sparks*

When I was old enough to get a job besides babysitting, my mom and I were in the local 5 & 10. My mom asked the owner, Judy, if she needed any help, she said yes! I was just thirteen years old, but she had high school kids in there working, and it was walking distance for me. So I started for $6 an hour cash. To me that was good money. I worked there for close to 6 years, and I learned so much.

Judy was a tough cookie and a shrewd business owner. She did not care what suggested retail price was, she knew her store offered convenience for our little town, so she added a few bucks on top of every MSRP. And the locals didn't mind paying more if it meant they could stay out of those big box stores up on the highway. Plus, she had a lot of variety, so kind of a one-stop-shop, you know. Oh we sold everything from plants, beach chairs, stationary, screws, to paint.

From Judy, I learned how to cut keys, mix paint, take inventory, the list went on and on. To this day, I always surprise people with my skills, because I have a general knack on most things home related—things most people never learn, way beyond just changing lightbulbs. I am so grateful for that! Eventually my brother and sister would also wind up working there as well. And that provided plenty of shenanigans in ways big and small, let me tell you.

Overall, though, the job was good and set a foundation for me when it came to working, paying bills, and running a business. It even made me think maybe one day I could own my own something. Who knew? My mom talked often about a 9 to 5, but there always had been that little entrepreneurial calling in me. I mean, look at Judy. Judy had been a teacher, but she left that job to buy this 5 & 10 from an elderly couple. Judy was sharp, knew so much, didn't need a man to run the hardware part.

Auto Parts, Filing Cabinets, and One Too Many Whistles

The 5 & 10 was great, but at nineteen I became pregnant with Jared. I needed a job with benefits, and a higher hourly wage. So my Uncle Ted got me a job at an automotive center. This was a whole new thing for me. My dad was a mechanic, so I did know a little bit about cars. And, my uncle would be working with me as a mechanic, so I could always ask him if I needed anything. So why not? Working for a corporation was fascinating to me. They were opening a new automotive store so I would now be doing 2 full weeks of training, soup to nuts on everything! I mean, I learned a lot in this position, too. At the 5 & 10, I learned about running a retail store. But here, I was learning even more about customer service from a corporate perspective. I mean, did you know when you answer the phone with a smile the other person can feel it? It's true. Try it! I loved the structure, the ideas, business concepts, the people…oh boy, I soaked it all in!

Soon enough, I was opening and closing the center myself. That's the thing about me, I dive full in to anything I do. My boss at the time, Jerry, was a great guy. He'd have BBQs in the back, buy us lunch, do all kinds of things to show appreciation and increase moral. I was once again blessed. They were good to me and I worked very hard for them to be the best employee I could be, because as we know, "get a 9-5" was my mom's staple saying. I thought I made it! Here I was just a high school graduate, working with people who were college educated, doing the same job as me, without student loans to pay back! I reached the holy grail, got my 9 to 5, and loved it.

Like any business, though, it had its rollercoaster moments. The company was short staffed in the back, so this cute mechanic named Pat volunteered to come down from his location (about a half hour away) and help us out. I mean he was getting paid the commute time, so he figured why not? We met the first day, and when he left for lunch I was surprised.

I mean he had just taken off, where could he have gone? He didn't live around here. How did he know where he was going? I thought for sure that would be my opportunity to help this guy out. But, no, he just went off to lunch without a word.

So the next day, it was lunch time, and I suggested I could show him where to go. I was penniless and didn't want him to think I was inviting myself so he could pay, so I told him I wasn't hungry. He took me up on my offer, insisted I have a slice of pizza, and so began this whirlwind relationship that led to marriage, kids, moving in and out of homes, and ending with a divorce and an estranged father. Didn't see all that coming from the cute mechanic, but you know how the story goes. I'll get into a few more details later, but not too much because I wouldn't want it to wind up in a country song.

Back to my point—see how a guy can totally run you off course? Anyhow, I stayed with the auto center for many years, I became very knowledgeable, and knew all the customers well. Many of our customers were car dealerships, and I guess I was pretty good at my job because the one customer from the "high end" dealership we worked with often said I should really come work for them. And one day it hit me, this guy was serious, I just needed to say the word.

I mean, what a tempting offer. To go work for this luxury car dealership would be a step up from my current 9 to 5. I mean wearing nice clothes, no more blue polo shirts, this was next level 9 to 5! My current, very kind boss encouraged me knowing it would be a better opportunity for me. I'm not sure I realized how selfless he was at the time, but I sure do now.

I went in for the interview and they offered me so much more, not being a corporation, they had flexibility. This seemed like such a golden opportunity, so I made my decision. I was going for it. My boss at the automotive center let me stay on at that current job to work on Sunday's just so I could keep the benefits I needed till the new ones kicked in. This meant working 7 days a week for a while, but it was worth it. I was providing health benefits for my family.

I began working at the luxury car dealer, with a glimmer of excitement to be in this kind of environment. But, oh boy, talk about being thrown into something, having to figure things out very quickly, AND in a male dominated environment again. There was so much I didn't know. I thought I needed way more knowledge and experience than I had, and I couldn't figure out (at first) why they even hired me??? But hey, I was hanging in there. I was working in the service department answering calls, making calls, filing, ringing and ringing and ringing up customers, selling jobs, taking care of the loaner cars…it was all a blur.

I had never even been inside a service center let alone know what the service center does! Honestly, my automotive center job was nothing like the pace of this one. Due to my lack of experience and young age, I didn't quite know how to juggle all the responsibilities they put on me, but I was grateful. Those people soon became like family early on. About a year after I began at the dealership Pat (that cute mechanic) and I got married, and most of my co-workers in the department even attended my wedding. We got along pretty well and enjoyed joking around in the slow times.

Our dealership prided themselves on outstanding customer service and boy we would do anything to get a good survey. The 3 gentleman I worked the front counter with were pros. They knew their stuff and they did their best to help me learn the ropes considering there was no formal training. It was a very demanding, fast-paced job with so many variables all of the time, but we all did our best.

Our little family-like environment though started to feel a bit muddied. No matter where I would be in the dealership, I would hear very uncomfortable conversations, and comments. Then slowly, things were indirectly said to me. Maybe I lived in a bubble, maybe I just let the words slip in one ear and out the other. Slowly, over time, I became more and more aware of exactly the things they said that were just not okay—on both ends of the spectrum. I mean men in every department as well as customers would comment on women's bodies, just plain old behaving badly.

Eventually it became too much. When I would walk in the garage at any point in time, I would simply dread it. You ask why? Well, I would hear that whistle and just know what was about to happen (not to mention the entire male mechanic staff). I would enter and the song "Brick House" would start to play loud enough to fill the entire 12 bay shop. Believe it or not, I didn't totally realize it for a while, but then putting two and two together, combined with the comments from all the other departments and customers—oh boy, I got it. I was so naive that I wasn't sure if it was a compliment or a bad thing. I'm still not sure actually. Maybe they thought they were complimenting me. Maybe I did kind of feel flattered but awkward at the same time. My solution was to use a technique that I am very good at it, just try to avoid it.

Oh yeah, rather than telling them to stop, because I wasn't completely sure it was about me, I would just find other doors to enter the dealership. I would sneak in through sides, walk in the back, try to not stand totally straight, basically try to hide a bit from it all. But you know what? Eventually, I ran out of options. Everyone knew, I only worked with 3 other women in my department, but they didn't enter the shop too often. They were close to twice my age and to my knowledge, no one was playing music about their bodies when they walked into the shop.

And then there was the whole workload thing. They gave me a lot of it. There were times I would be filing, and at least once a week I noticed that my front desk colleagues never ever had to file. I worked on commission, so losing 1 day a week took a toll on my potential earnings. And it was just me, doing the filing for the service department even though I technically was the only service writer with this added responsibility. Guess that goes back to me being naive, and being responsible for many jobs, but just not realizing it at the time.

Here's the kicker, at one point some generic training material came across my hand in VHS format mind you. I saw a class on "Sexual Harassment." Hmm. Interesting. I suggested to my direct boss and he said sure order it, go for it. So now I was also responsible to "train" the dealership. They would come in, in shifts to watch the outdated video, sign that they watched said video, then case closed. Training complete. I thought the sexual harassment video might open some people's eyes, but nope. Nada. Unfortunately even watching that didn't change things. I felt there was nothing left to do.

Observing, listening to all these things, I was almost immune to the catcalls by this point. But it didn't just happen to me. This was the culture. The environment was filled with this kind of talk. I decided to start keeping a journal of all the improper things said by staff to each other, about customers, in the shop to me etc. I was like a scene out of a show. I was totally aware of everything, now, and I knew it wasn't right. So, I would write little Post-it notes throughout the day. It wasn't obvious to anyone, really. I just wanted to write reminders for me, and then I would log them in to my journal. It was wild. So many people participated in it and some just stayed out of it. But nobody stopped it. And, this sexual talk was everywhere, even with some of the customers who would take part in it.

Now, at my previous automotive job, I do remember a specific conversation that was completely inappropriate, but it was just once. At this supposedly high-end luxury dealer, the conversations never stopped. I didn't care how much money these people made or the positions they held, nothing was worth feeling like this. So one day, when I was outside filing AGAIN, (even though at this point, I was a full-fledged, qualified service writer I was still made to file weekly every single ticket that happened that previous week) my co-worker who was in charge of the shop said something with a sexual connotation in regard to attire, body, and "whale tails." Well, that was the last straw. At that point I had had it. I'd been there as a great employee for several years, but I just lost it. That was the end. I couldn't take it anymore—everything was so wrong. At one point, I even consulted a lawyer but when she mentioned wearing a wire and becoming involved in a sting operation, I had enough. Instead, I just quit.

Family Matters and Figuring It Out

By this time, Pat and I were married, raising 4 kids, and needed both of our incomes to make ends meet. I quit abruptly, but I thought that since I was leaving a prestigious position at a "good company," I would easily find another job. I needed a job ASAP—there was no way I couldn't work. I provided financially for our family. We had a mortgage we already couldn't afford. No worries, right? I figured I'd just figure it out like I always do, but oh, man, the pressure.

My husband really didn't care either way. I mean he wasn't running over to burn the dealership down or kick some ass, but he wasn't mad that I up and quit either. My mother, on the other hand, well, let's just say my mother was furious by all that went on at the dealership, especially this one guy who was the worst. I swear she would have driven right through their fancy glass windows to hurt him if I'd let her. Of course, I didn't. I did see him in the mall a few years later while I was shopping with her, and no joke, she wanted to seriously hurt him! She can be a firecracker when protecting her family, that's for sure.

So here I was a married mother of 4, with no money in the bank and a pile of bills to pay. We got stuck in that mortgage scheme going around in 2006—you may remember where banks were giving money to people like us who had none and qualifying us for a mortgage nearly double our first home, that there was NO WAY we could keep up with. We were so naive, we believed the lender, but we were all kinds of upside down with money. Now I had just quit my job because I could not take it anymore and so I couldn't even file for unemployment. I wasn't sure what exactly would happen, but I was trusting that this happened for a reason. I didn't want to go back to the automotive industry, although my resume was most impressive there. Instead I applied for retail positions, only to find out my desired hourly rate (on the low end) was what a manager would make!!! Ugh. A regular retail position paid half that, and no one would hire me as a manager without real retail experience. I had no time to "work my way up." Oh boy. How was I going to do this?

Despite all my financial troubles, I would put all that junk aside and go to regular mass every Sunday. Swallowing my pride a bit, I would casually mention that I was looking for work— even though I didn't know it, I guess I was good at networking, it's just who I am! But at this point I needed to find a job badly. You see, to complicate matters even worse, just days after leaving the dealership, I got a call from my gynecologist.

"Jessica," the doctor said in a low tone, "we need to have a talk. Your annual test results came back."

I nearly dropped the phone. It was a mess. More of a mess than just up and quitting my job, now my health was crashing, too. There I was, now unemployed, and having to have a hysterectomy. I guess it was a good thing I wasn't working now, right? But this just seemed to be the lightning bolt in the middle of my shitstorm.

It turns out I didn't have a choice—I had to have either a partial or full hysterectomy done because my cells were pre-cancerous. It was pretty serious. Once again, being young and naive, I just did what the doctor suggested at the time. No second opinion. No weighing my options. My doctor recommended a partial, and so I had the partial hysterectomy done at 28 years old, with a 6-week recovery time. If I can teach you one thing from this book, it's to speak up! You've got a voice. Ask questions. You don't have to just do as the doctor says all of the time. I mean, if I thought more about it, maybe I would have done a full hysterectomy.

After the procedure, I did my best to just rest, stay still and do nothing. Now that's a pretty big deal, because anyone that knows me knows that is just not part of my nature. So I did my best. The good news was that they caught it early enough, and I had 4 beautiful healthy kids. I was so fortunate but when you get that call, the world looks different.

Everything seemed so much more real, more precious. I remember driving down Grassmere Avenue in Interlaken and just being fascinated by the designs and colors of everything from the landscape to the architecture to the nature surrounding it all. Now mind you I've been on that street probably a million times by that point in my life!! I can't believe all of the things you notice when you think you are short on time. If only we could live like that every day. So present, so still, so connected. I'm always going but this sure did force me to slow down and take a moment.

Then of course, seeing how life can turn on a dime, I added a new life insurance policy for my kids. I felt better knowing they would have some sort of security, since things can change so quickly and you have to adapt quickly, "bend don't break," they say. I was doing my best.

Make It Your Business to Keep It Moving, Sister

Learn from Everyone

There is absolutely something you can learn from everyone who is put in your path. Sometimes we learn what we want and other times we learn what we don't, but always there is knowledge to be gained. Even if you don't agree with someone's actions, remember they were placed in your life for a reason. Take the lesson and use it to help yourself and others in the future.

Use Your Gut as Your Guide

If something feels off, it probably is! Listen to your gut when it's telling you something isn't right. Know your worth and stand up for it. No amount of money is worth your self-esteem, and when you listen to your gut it won't steer you wrong. I was scared as heck leaving that job at the luxury car dealership, but it played an important role in my life that led me to exactly where I was meant to be!

Money Isn't Worth Your Sanity

Listen, we all need to pay our bills. I get it. But too often you hear of women staying in jobs that drain them. Whether it be like me, with sexual harassment, or with overbearing bosses, or with a job that doesn't use all of their skills. Whatever the reason, money is not worth your peace of mind, your sanity, or your integrity. When you walk away from something or someone that doesn't value you, you are only making space for something or someone who does.

Appreciate Your One and Only Precious Life

As cliché as it sounds, life really is precious. Don't let a health scare be the reason you notice the world around you. Make every moment count. Take a deep breath and take it all in. And don't forget those annual appointments—see your doctors, your dentist, get those screenings, and always take care of you because that's something no one else can do.

CHAPTER
Six

Gifts, Hoarders, and Getting WIP'd Into Business

"Your talent is God's gift to you. What you do with it is your gift back to God."
~ *Leo Buscaglia*

So after I had the surgery and recovered, I was looking and applying for jobs anywhere I could. But these jobs were not even paying $10 an hour!? How could we survive on that? After taxes it was just pennies, and my ex-husband didn't make enough to cover the expenses, the house was going under foreclosure, and I needed to find somewhere to live that I knew the kids and I wouldn't be locked out of at any point in time. I know I mentioned the foreclosure part before—I don't want to bore you with too many details, you get that I was broke, right? Yes, we were in one heck of a financial situation. So I quit my job at the worst possible time, or best, depending on how you look at it. I mean, looking back, the marriage was not working foreclosure or not. This just got me to move us all out a little sooner.

One day after church, Father Bill was standing there in the back, and I casually said, "Father Bill, if you ever need some help, let me know."

He looked interested but didn't say much in the moment. I needed to work, and he knew my situation—the looming divorce, foreclosure, and lack of a job. So Father Bill got back to me about a week later and said the church programs could help me with a down payment for a security deposit. Plus, he told me they desperately needed some new and young blood for their annual dinner dance which, in its heyday, was a smashing success. He explained that now the committee members were older, much older than me, and tired of all the work that went into it. They were still committed to it but committed pretty much to the least amount of effort they needed to make it happen, hence it not being as successful.

Saving Grace and the Start of Something Big

Father Bill proposed I work in the after-school program they had in the basement, which was free to the local community kids of Asbury Park, and also fundraise for the annual dinner dance. I wasn't exactly sure what that meant, I mean the school had asked for donations at times, but that's all I really knew. So of course I said YES, why not? I am always up for a good challenge and getting that dance back to its prime would be fulfilling, helpful to the church, and teach me another skill. I would learn anything I needed to along the way as I always did, and I would give it my all, and do my very best. I would rock it even though I wasn't sure what that meant.

I'm happy to report that I did in fact figure it out along the way. There were no directions or "get this dance off the ground manuals." It was basically, "You're in, great! Good luck with that."

I just began with what I knew. People. So I wrote and mailed hundreds if not thousands of letters. First I wrote a letter and sent it out to every single person I knew and asked them to attend the dinner dance. It was a hefty price tag for some at $60 per person but I had 60 people say YES! The dance had never had a higher attendance.

Next I cracked open the PHONE book, yes I said it! I went through all of the letters in the alphabet, and I sent out the traditional letter asking for donations from companies that I thought would be a good fit. The church secretary had never seen anything done like that before but kept me loaded up with letters, envelopes, and stamps. Any spare moment I had I was addressing envelopes, even while sitting at my son's football practice, just going and going. Not letting up. Donations came pouring in in the form of gift certificates or coupons or even the occasional gift. Some sent letters back requesting I come pick up the donation, which of course, I did. The blessings were flowing, so when it was all said and done there were over 100 baskets!! The large majority being the ones I collected.

The night was incredible, and I had decided that I would

not work that night. I sat, danced, and enjoyed my first ever Harvest Moon Dinner Dance surrounded by so many loved ones that were there to support me.

So even though you might not know exactly what you're doing take a chance, put yourself out there, and ask for help. You've totally got this.

Another part of working at the church was helping run the after-school program and meeting some lifelong friends. Antonia would clean homes all day and then head right over to the basement to start her work there. Then there was Tami, a very kind mother of 9. We became so close, almost like sisters. You'll learn all about her a bit later.

All in all, this time in my life was transformational. In that church, God planted many seeds—in my friendships and in my business and how I could tie a business into the good work these amazing women were doing in the basement. I had no clue just how much of an impact this church job would have, but let me tell you, it all began with a question Sister Jude asked me while I was working in the after-school program, "Do you think you could help me organize my office?"

I said sure, although I wasn't totally sure what that meant but I would figure it out. I guess you see the pattern with me. Say yes first, figure out how later. Sister Jude was in charge of a K-8 Catholic school serving predominantly low-income families, who come from various backgrounds. She did this all by herself; essentially, she was in charge of everything, and would also teach Math to the older kids. Sister Jude got the job and the previous principal's "stuff" was still everywhere in the office. So while Sister Jude is a no-nonsense type of person and likes to cut to the chase, I did my best to make it as simple as I could.

Oh boy, did I figure it out.

At one point she even said to me, "What you have is a gift, it's not that everyone doesn't want to be organized it's just that some people just don't know how to do it."

The seed was planted. She said those words to me in such a way, that they hit me right in my heart. Was it a gift? Was it my gift? I never thought of it like that. Then I watched an episode of Hoarders. Was this another sign? I knew I could do it. Maybe people did need help organizing. Maybe it was my gift. I was always an organized kid. And I took that on as an extra add-in with almost any job I had. I just needed things to be in order, or I'd twitch. Gift or neurosis, whatever you want to call it. If people would pay for this service, maybe this was my business.

Through working at the church, I was able to find a nice, quaint rental home for me and the kids. My ex and I were separated, waiting on the divorce to be finalized, and I just knew I would need more income, especially as the kids got older. I knew he wasn't going to be able to give child support. And Sister Jude's words to me along with all these little signs, I had to get the opinion of the ladies I admired so much as business leaders.

So, I was hosting the WIP monthly meeting at my small rental home in December 2010. The weather was not great. Snow covered the roads. But the core group still showed up.

At the end of each meeting, one member could take the floor and use 3 to 4 minutes of time to pose a question to the group.

I was stepping into my power. It was a big thing for me to even be hosting this thing. So I decided to go all in—this was also my night to use my voice, and I had my question ready—I was going to ask, "Is there really a need for this thing called a home organizer?"

I had been thinking about this and keeping it inside, waiting for this moment. It was completely swirling in my head and my heart was beating out of my chest. I was so ready to ask the ladies (who I respected and admired) their opinions. What if they laughed? What if they thought I was not qualified for this? I didn't go to college. I didn't take a course in organization. But just like me, the girl who had no business, I asked anyway. I just went for it!

And guess what? They all answered a resounding yes! Half of them hired me on the spot before I knew about anything. Then Veera called out, "If you can do my kitchen you can do anything!"

Are you kidding me? Challenge accepted, girl. I was nervous but excited! The group stressed the importance of before and after pictures, note taken.

So it was at that point just a few evenings later, I was heading down to Point Pleasant to organize Veera's kitchen. I could not believe it. I was doing my first real organizing job, outside of Sister Jude, of course, in a doctor's home no less. Did I mention that? Veera is actually Dr. Veera, and she is brilliant, kind, generous, but totally straightforward and direct. I had to be totally prepared.

So in the days leading up to that first job, I dove right in and started to do some online research on home organizers—what they did, rates, structure. I was shocked to find out that the spectrum of rates was $50-$200 an hour. Uh, holy crap. Really??

So I arrived at Veera's second floor walk-up, and we went to town. It just came completely natural to me. It was kind of instinctual. Veera and her fiancé were both extremely busy in their work lives and very active travelers, so the kitchen needed a little TLC, but who could blame them? When you finally do have down time, who the heck wants to organize anything???

So there I was on a chair going through cans and jars of expired food tossing it left and right. Then wiping up the cabinets and figuring out a usable system for what remained. The evening just flowed right through me, almost felt effortless. I think I got that from my mom, by the way. On the occasion we would visit the emergency room of the hospital where she worked, everything would be neat, orderly and labeled. I don't even think that was part of her job, she just enjoyed it. It came naturally to her. Eventually it did become her job by the way. A perfect fit.

So back to the kitchen, within a few hours, we had bags and bags leaving her place and out the door. Donations, trash…Oh my, it was a beautiful thing and so freeing. Tons of work with all those stairs, but it was awesome. Getting in and getting it done.

Amazing.

I was a professional organizer.

My clients were so happy, so happy in fact, I went back several times to do each room, even the attic! They were hooked to the organizational feeling and look. Just to report the couple got married, moved to a new home, and I am still going as often as I can get over there.

After that first night organizing, I was so confident and full of ideas. I wanted to organize anyone's home I could get my hands on. I felt like a new woman with a newfound wave of possibility. $10 an hour, what? You know it's only up from here. So, I followed up with everyone that showed interest and made those appointments. I had come up with a price point of $50 an hour but started with the "friends and family" discount on day 1 because I didn't feel comfortable charging $50 an hour to those I knew. It just seemed like a lot of money. I was rocking and rolling, though, helping out friends and family to build my portfolio and resume, and of course, took those before and afters.

Collecting Seeds Along the Way

At this time, in the evenings and Saturday nights when the kids would go with my ex-husband, I would just spend hours and hours researching this whole concept on the computer wedged in between the wall and TV cabinet. I had never, and I mean NEVER, done so much research on anything in my life.

Home organizing was really a thing, it wasn't terribly

known or popular but there were people doing it successfully for years. I mean this was way before anyone had ever heard about "The Life Changing Magic of Tidying Up" and Marie Kondo. These organizers were the pioneers, and if it hadn't been that random show Hoarders on that random night, I may have never even thought about it ever. But hey, one of my favorite sayings is, "nothing is random or pure chance."

At that time in my life the kids were 12, 9, 6 & 4. I was working in the afternoons, a few hours for the church and school, and then right to the after-school program directly after my church shift. I really enjoyed being in and working in the church. Organizing closets, running errands, writing postcards, making the bingo schedule, and trying my best to find a working computer and printer in the school. These inner-city kids were cared about by every last person that worked in any capacity in that small Catholic school. I've witnessed close near miracles of kindness there. It was a true gift to work in that environment, one that shaped me in ways nothing else could have, and inspired ideas in me that have become founding principles for my company as it is today.

Shortly after I started entertaining the idea of making the organizing thing a real go, the after-school programs merged with the two churches, and then even merged again to include another charter school thanks to a generous grant and lots of hard work. Everyone really cared about all of these students, and we did the best we could do each and every day. Whether it be by giving them healthy snacks, helping the kids with homework, providing good experiences, or just doing fun activities with them, we cared about their well-being even through the challenges they had sometimes given us.

I remember one day when it really hit home for me. It was back when I had just begun my first year at the afterschool program. I was given the cool room in the corner, and I would be responsible for the kindergarten class. I was only a few days in and yes I had the cute little tables and chairs, but the toys were sparse at best. The kids would come into my class, sometimes in their pj shirts and just be so happy with what little we did have in there.

Something didn't feel right.

Here my kids didn't have that "much," but they had a lot more than these children did. My daughter Reilly and son Damian were sharing a small room in our rental on Garven with the stackable washer and dryer in one closet and some clothes and toys in the other. I was moved to action. That plastic kitchen that we had gotten from someone that they never played with anymore was now placed directly in my minivan along with ½ of the toys they owned. Yes, I said HALF. But guess what? My kids didn't even care!

Then I became obsessed with this concept of giving what is no longer used, appreciated, or celebrated. Who would have known, what it was like for these kids? Of course you hear stories, but I witnessed the lack first hand. And I thought we were struggling.

Can you say it was almost like Christmas morning the next day in my classroom?! The kids were in awe of all these new things to play with, they were so happy! I have to say in that moment, I made a choice. I would live a minimalist life, and minimalism was more than a buzz word to me. You bet, in that one moment, I made the decision, and my kids would never know indulgence, even if it was to a small degree, again. I began to spread the word and put it out there for people to understand.

True, real life stories—people were curious and interested. They wanted to know more of this phenomenon taking place in the basement of the church. They wanted their kids to donate their unloved possessions and some even wanted to see this operation for themselves. It was amazing and one of the core parts of my business from that lesson in the church basement. Seeds planted for sure.

So here I was working for the church doing auction stuff, organizing the ongoing donations, tidying the bathrooms, then helping the kids do their homework, bringing in snacks, cleaning out their backpacks, and just loving every moment, even the difficult ones.

With this new "organizing" I needed to find the time. I wanted to make a go of it.

In the mornings before work at the school, evenings, and weekends, I would set up appointments to organize for anyone that would let me practice and some even paid me. I was just going by something I felt. I could do this, and there was a need. Clutter and disorganization leads to lots of stress, for moms especially. And all that stuff that people no longer love and need has another home just waiting for it, people who could use it, and will be so grateful for it. Was organizing homes and donating the excess a lot on top of everything else I was doing? Sure it was, but I just felt that it would be worth it.

I started to fill an envelope with cash so I could save on the side. My oldest son was going to be turning 13 in December. I wanted him to have an unforgettable 13th birthday trip, and this just might be the way to make it happen.

Things were working out and going well. I began to think that I was going to make this side hustle official. I was loving this home organizing concept. I had gotten so confident in my ability I figured I would need headshots for this new business. So in February, I bartered services for a woman to take professional photos of me. This would be my very first headshot in my 31 years of life. Posted the pictures, along with some testimonials, and all in all, upped my game. And by April, I had 12 clients!! They all were different but essentially wanted order in their disorder.

Making This Thing a Real Thing

April of 2011, I made an appointment with a family friend named Claudio, who was a lawyer. We sat together in his office in West Long Branch and opened the LLC that I still have to this day. I'm forever grateful for his wise guidance and hand-holding techniques that have saved me over and over again. I walked into his office not having a clue in the world what I was actually doing or what it entailed at that time. The most important thing for me was that I had just enough money to cover the fees associated with opening my LLC. He did his best to advise, guide, lead and fill out the application for the naive girl with wide eyes that sat across from him that day.

Did you know that organizing can save someone from losing their family home?

It's true, we did it. A woman in Long Branch (through a friend of a friend) found out about my new service and reached out. Her family home was in great disrepair and full of items she held so dear, some of which most people would never understand. I mean there were piles of plastic bags on the floor, Campbell's soup cans and jelly jars strewn on tables, drawers too stuffed to close with lint rollers and flashlights and Ziplocks protruding from the top. Potholders and vitamin bottles mixed with lamps and spoons—let's just say nothing had a proper place and walking through her home had become a bit of a maze, potentially hazardous. I could see her just hanging in and holding on. It was so bad that the state was getting involved with the situation. It had to be cleared, and come to find out, the state would pay for our services to help her with the clearing.

We worked for weeks. I had employed my oldest son and my mother to help. The job was enormous with every nook and cranny of the home clutter free and packed. We removed over 150 black bags of items that were completely unusable. It was an incredible transformation. You could now walk in and through the house, completely down the stairs to the basement, and out the door.

After understanding the situation a little more, I realized this all began because the woman was about to lose her home.

She couldn't keep up with the mortgage. Then I met Rob Lowe at a networking event. Not the famous Rob Lowe— although that would have been awfully cool. It was Rob Lowe the reverse mortgage specialist. Together Rob and I essentially saved this woman from losing her very dear family home. Oh how rewarding.

In July, I had moved up in the world literally, to the penthouse! I was now doing my first packing, overseeing, and unpacking job. Did I really know what I was doing 100%??? NO!! But you bet I figured it out along the way. Another update this Client #22 is still with us as we go to her every other week for 6 hours at a clip. She's a successful attorney, with teenage kids and no time. She thrives at work helping people, so we help her at home.

So closing out my first year I had assisted 32 clients and made just over $8,000. I couldn't believe that I could make money like that around a schedule that was flexible. I started to think I would want to help women in my situation, single mothers possibly with no child support or in an array of circumstances, live better and help others through organizing. Another seed planted.

And amazingly, in December of 2011, I had made enough side money to take my oldest Jared to Cancun Mexico for his 13th birthday. Jared and I got our first passports in the same year. I wanted my children to get out and see the world sooner rather than later as I had. 13 vs 31. We had a beautiful time and learned a bit about traveling together.

Growing Pains and Hiring Help

In my second year, I kept going to some of my existing clients. They were in love with the organizational feel, so I kept going back and back to them. Meanwhile they were telling their friends about my company. You know, the company that would come and do all these cool things in their home?!

Word spread and next thing you know their friends wanted in on this magic. There were a few instances when I needed to call in an extra set of hands or two for the larger jobs. That's where my mom and oldest son would come in. Every job was different, and I didn't always know how I would get it done, but I always did, and the clients were so grateful!

During this year, I was even asked to start speaking about organizational issues. Oh, wow. My friends were clearly professional and gifted speakers, and here I was with my homemade bright orange poster board with "before and after" photos I had scotch-taped right on the board. PowerPoint, heck no! I was DIY, homemade, make it work all the way. And I'm not talking cute Pinterest-y DIY. I mean old school on the cheap DIY. I had absolutely no idea what I was doing but I was doing it! And I guess that's just the way I roll.

But, come to think of it, I never did hear an unkind word about my truly homemade presentation tri-folds. I think people don't care as much as you think. I mean we put all this pressure on ourselves to be perfect, but, as long as you have good information that's really helpful to them, they don't care about the fancy stuff.

So, no it wasn't easy juggling a few jobs, kids, and a life but I knew this organizing deal could and would work. So much so, that I knew in my heart very early on that I wanted to eventually franchise Organize By Design to help women in similar situation as my own, so they could make money and yet still be around for their children. Work 20 hours a week, take my kids to their activities, be a troop leader, heck yeah! I'll have some of that!

Forget this working 4 jobs around the clock struggling nonsense, I had a taste of something more with the seeds that had been planted since I was a little girl. I knew my company would not only help women, but all the people whose lives we better organized, and all the people who received the donations. Take over the world, you say? I was ready, even though I was clueless as to how to do all that. No big deal, I knew I'd figure it out.

I did share the idea of franchising with a few people. Most just listened, a few kind of encouraged me, but one woman in particular that I very much admired said, "How would you do it? It could never be done."

Sadly, I believed her and buried that idea deep down inside. Since I thought she was smarter than me, I assumed she must be right.

That's the thing about dreams. You should share them, but you can't let people squash them. I look back and think the time wasn't right then, and I'm so grateful I didn't bury that dream so deep that it stayed down there. But the squashing does happen to way too many dreamers like me.

I rounded out 2012 with 55 clients and just about doubled my previous year's numbers.

As you can see, slowly but surely, this business was working, because after about 2 years into it, I no longer had time to do 20 hours at my part-time job, so we reduced it to 10 hours and then I couldn't even commit to that, so they just kept me at the school on an "as needed" basis. Eventually, I had to stop that even.

Sister Jude understood and supported me. She's the one who encouraged me to use this gift! I did love the school and the students there, but I was being called into a new direction. And you better believe still to this day, when something is donated that the school can use, it's theirs! For example, one client had gym balls, dozens of them, in all colors, and he thought no one would possibly use them. Well, wouldn't you know I made a quick call to the school and they were delighted! Oh, boy, they could definitely use them! Dozens and dozens of unused coloring books—why yes, I have a place. What a blessing.

And year after year, we grew. I learned how to deal with new challenges, like when Hurricane Sandy hit, and no items were salvageable. I had to help people who just lost everything find peace after the storm, even though I know inside they were shattered. I wanted to help people to the best of my ability. I realized that if I did want this to be a thing, I could not do it all alone or only call in my family as needed. I actually needed to hire help, like for real.

You see, I was on a job in Wayside, going from the basement

to the top floor, up and down—didn't I tell you organizing was hard work? For the life of me, I couldn't catch my breath. It was completely bizarre. I did not understand it. So of course, I finished the job anyway, and that evening I decided to go to the emergency room. Well after a chest x-ray my shortness of breath made sense. I found out I had pneumonia in the middle of the summer. It hit me like a cinderblock. I couldn't continue like this anymore.

So when I was better, I began to ask around for anyone that knew anyone that might consider working for me. My dear friend Lesly referred me to my very first real employee. I hired her referral, and she went on tons of jobs with me, so she would know just what to do, and of course she had a knack for it on her own.

But, you know, I really did not like to let my "baby" go. It was way harder than you'd think. Eventually I did start sending her out alone and it was working out great. Next thing you know I hired another woman and I trained her in half the time because I already did it once before, AND she was amazing.

Things were going better than I could have imagined! I even began to work with a business coach who saw enormous potential in my company. She shared ideas with me grander than my biggest desire, and she was an intelligent woman who graduated from Wharton. I mean she knew her stuff! I was on fire, someone could see and actually put on paper what I saw. She believed in me, and that was priceless.

I held my first team dinner for the 3 of us. It was all coming together. We were happy, and the business was taking shape!

Meeting so many people, helping them organize their homes AND their lives, I even had an idea for a book. But while I love reading books, writing is not really my strong point, so I found a co-author who lived for writing!! I'll tell you all about that later.

We spent months together, writing and discussing all types of organizational stories. I mean why not? Closing out the year with 121 clients and making more money that year then I had since I had left the luxury car dealer, just by organizing. I was making the income I needed and providing a way for 2 other women to earn money.

I felt like I hit the lottery! Talk about jackpot! I was helping my clients, helping the environment, helping the women working for me, helping families in need, and supporting my family. Now that's a win win-win.

Make It Your Business to Use Your Gifts

Remember There is an Answer to Every Question

Yes, you read that right! You can solve any problem, figure out any situation, do whatever you put your heart and mind to. We make anything out of our immediate realm of knowledge seem far scarier than it is, that we stay stuck in our comfort zones for way longer than our ticket there is meant for. For me, just knowing I can figure stuff out gives me courage. Also, knowing all things are possible gives me greater faith. Heck yeah, you know we can all beat the odds even with all the cards stacked against us!

Listen to What Others Have to Say

Sometimes people can see things that we just can't. I'm not talking about the haters. I mean people who see the awesome things we do and tell us about them. We give each other clues all the time about the things we admire in one another. This will lead you directly to your gift. Don't brush off that your best friend thinks you're ubercreative or that your son's teacher thinks you are a great listener. Maybe your gift will lead you to do interior design, or life coaching, or personal shopping. The sky is the limit my friend. Let others lead you there if you can't see it for yourself.

Don't Wait for Perfect

Perfection paralysis is a real problem. And I understand how much you want to have enough money, enough information, enough customers before beginning something new. But, the problem with that is there really is no such thing as "perfect." And so waiting for it is futile. If I waited for everything to be perfect before I started my organization company, I'd still be waiting! Just dive in and get going, your gifts can't wait for someone to receive them! Whether you use your gifts to start a business, a side hustle, or to donate in service of others, the time is NOW.

Delegate and Teach Others

Nothing phenomenal has ever been built solo. It takes a team, a village, a group of people with the same mission in mind. In other words, you can't do this alone, my friend. You are going to reach a point when in order to grow and share your gifts with even more people, you're going to have to delegate some stuff and teach other people how to do the things that you do so you don't end up passing out in the emergency room. The best part about delegating is that you allow other people the space to use their gifts, and that is beyond empowering!

CHAPTER
Seven

Snafus, Heartbreaks, and Building an Empire

"No one gets to tell you how big your dreams can be." ~ Rachel Hollis

I had a feeling pretty early on in my business that I wanted to grow it and help other women like me be able to work 4 hours a day and still pay their bills and be at their kid's soccer games. I also knew I was helping so many people. My formula was simple: go into the home, identify what needed to go, find another home for it and donate it to those who could use it, recycle what needed to be recycled, properly dispose of what needed to be disposed. I was teaching so many people the value of minimalism, living with only what you love, long before Marie Kondo was telling everyone to only keep items that spark joy. Girl, I get it!

So seeing my company grow and being able to employ

people, help charities, and make my clients super happy was a dream come true. In 2015, I hired another woman who was a natural organizer, Alli. Organize By Design was working so well, the clients were increasing, and lots were returning for more time with us. Heck yeah, we were on to something. We were offering a high-level service that many people needed and we served them 100%. It was that year we had one of our first newspaper articles written on us! The phone was ringing, and I felt like a real entrepreneur.

I had met a friend (you will learn all about her later), Jenn, and she mentioned partnering with larger companies to add value through my expertise. What?! So crazy because I thought about working with bigger companies, but this was not something I knew anything about. She planted a little seed for me, and I started to think of companies that might want to partner with me. In my line of work I used a ton of big black bags (for garbage, donations, etc.), I mean so many you would not even believe it.

An idea came to me. What if I could teach people my method of organizing, re-homing and donating items through a partnership with a larger company? This would give the company some value-added content for their customers and provide me a bigger platform to share my expertise. Bingo, exactly what Jenn told me about! I decided to reach out to this HUGE corporation myself—the one who manufactured the garage bags my company had used from day one—to suggest I be their brand ambassador, for this "envelope of hope" campaign I created, using their bags as the vehicle of transportation holding inside the donations to people in need. My dear friend Natalie saw what I was trying to do and so eloquently helped me write it all up in an email with my new contact in R&D of this major company!! We went back and forth for literally months. This was big time.

I pictured how many people we could inspire. I really believed in this idea and thought it could help me get to that next level. Another win-win-win. I was so full of hope and then even more ideas came to me. I couldn't wait to share about this huge partnership because in my mind, it was so happening. How could they say no?

A Hard Lesson and a Dose of No

Finally after all the back and forth, in the end I was told I was too big of a liability and it just couldn't be done. They did not hire me as a brand ambassador. Now I made friends with people who worked for that company, and one of them told me, "Jessica, I just want to let you know you have gone farther up the pole with your idea then any other marketing company has ever gone, and you should be very proud of yourself." I guess I was proud. I was so honored, I mean for him to say that after all our working together over the 6 months. I think he was disappointed it didn't get approved, too.

Fast forward a few months, I'm in a beautiful large master closet in Rumson with my near empty box of bags. I grabbed my new box of bags from my supply kit when something caught my eye. Oh boy. I lost all my air and began to see stars.

My trusty reliable garbage bag company had switched up the design of their box and now it included a little value-added marketing message.

Wait for it…

"Good for donations, parties, moving and remodeling." The Words were accompanied by a cute picture—it was all just so similar to my pitch.

Are you freaking kidding me??

I was so hurt and upset. They essentially took my whole idea and left me out to dry. It was everything from our months of meetings, from my beautifully worded email (thanks again, Natalie!), and everything from my heart. They took it all. And I immediately called BS that I was a liability. I just could not believe that could happen. I've heard about the cutthroat world of corporate but seriously? I never experienced it like this, just seemed so terrible. I could never do that to anyone no matter how big I grew, and I made a promise that one day, when I am in the market for brand ambassadors, I would never do anything like this. The timing and the ideas, all too much for a simple coincidence. The sad part of all of this was it happened at a time when I was on the upswing and small as it may seem to an outsider, it really felt like a pin to my balloon. It deflated me. It even made me question if I wanted to keep growing. It made me think I was too small.

Isn't it crazy how you can have all of these amazing validations, happy clients, awesome employees, articles in newspapers, and one damn big corporate giant can roll along and squash you? It happens all the time—we give our power away. Why do we do that? Well I had to put my big girl pants on and NOT allow one experience break my stride. I did call a few intellectual property attorneys, but they all said I'd get buried in legal fees. I decided none of that was worth it. Besides, one day they will be begging me to be a brand ambassador, and I will have my Pretty Woman moment, "Remember me? Big mistake. Huge."

Oh, that makes me smile.

So long story short, I got back up, moved forward, and continued building this empire. 2016 was in full swing. I had several women working for me, and some part-time as needed. It was a beautiful thing. Yes, there were some tougher, bigger jobs but we always got through them. And Holy Toledo, we won "Best Professional Organizer" by Monmouth Health and Life, a well-respected magazine in our area. What an honor! Not to mention it was in that year where we donated our millionth item. We had our biggest revenue jump to date. Things were good.

Restructuring, Growing Pains, and a Name Change To Boot

The following year, my company, Organize By Design was restructuring, and my 2 key employees at the time were not exactly thrilled with this. As a natural entrepreneur, change is exciting to me. But to people who value stability, change can be scary. One of the two had decided it was her time to go, so she quit. The other was no longer a good fit for the company,

I knew in my heart I had to let her go as hard as it would be without them both. I wasn't sure how I was going to be able to keep the pace, but my good close friends encouraged me and had my back 10000%. One in particular had suggested I would do even better!

And it's crazy but sometimes what we hold on to actually weighs us down. By releasing the people who were no longer gung ho for my company, it actually made room for people who were. Boy, my friend was right. That year Organize By Design had landed our largest 3-week, 3 person team job. It was massive! Of course it was not easy, but we did it. The before and after photos would blow you away. It still gives me chills.

The jobs were coming in, staffing was a challenge, and we had growing pains. I didn't have a good training system, so I just threw people in on jobs with me. I could never leave because I was the one who knew all the systems. I spent a ton of time marketing, networking, trying to grow the business even more. I figured I could hire people to help me with the infrastructure once I had enough revenue to sustain the help. It kind of was a never-ending circle and a lot of questioning, "What comes first, chicken or the egg?" type of thing.

The franchise or pod or licensing idea was so real in my heart. So that summer, after much tossing and turning, I just knew the name Organize By Design could not go to the scale of where I envisioned it. I mean, if you google Organize By Design there are many of them already. I kind of named my company on the fly when I first began, not doing enough research and certainly not thinking about growth such as this. But it was time. The name of the company would have to change. I was so nervous, I had worked so hard. I loved our logo, our orange business cards, and our reputation was so good. I worked hard with my team to build that brand. Organize By Design is all we were known by.

But the tug in my heart was real. It had to change. Now, mind you, our website never really brought in business, so it's not like the URL was hopping. And although the company was well-known locally, people knew me as the owner of it. They could find it just by looking me up, right? And I could set up forwarders online. But still, it was scary. Finally with the support of a friend, I was back at the high caliber marketing company that I was at in 2011. Now, I've known the owner for a long time, she was one of the original founders of WIP, so I was excited to share how far I'd come. And her team knew their stuff. So I hired them to help come up with a new available name and URL, then design the logo. It was surreal my vision was resurfacing. It had seen sunlight again, it was here. After a discovery session and research on the company's part, they presented us with a few names to choose from. I knew right away, the name that stood out, the new name of my company…

Organista Home!

It felt right, I so loved the new name. And thanks to two dear friends, Natalie and Amy – you know Natalie has a way with words already and Amy has a masters in English, she's a teacher, and an avid reader–lucky me! Two friends who are total wordsmiths, the same two friends that helped me with my first tagline, helped me with the new one..."Conquer Clutter & Embrace Space." Don't you just love it?

Then the logo was created, which came out absolutely perfect. They kept my signature orange but elevated my game big time. I was in love! But, I was frozen in fear too! For some unexplained reason I wasn't ready for the massive change, at least not then. I kept making excuses as to why now was not the right time. On the backend, we started working on a new website, but had no plans to put it out there any time soon. I just kept operating as Organize By Design and it was fine. That year the business revenue wise stayed about the same. We had grown in new clients but had plateaued from a revenue standpoint. It was okay. What's so nuts is that the plateau was a sign, but I couldn't see it. The plateau was the Universe telling me it's time to shift. And let me tell you, fear will stop the flow of money dead in its tracks, that's for sure.

Opportunity Knocks and Favors Returned

I decided that with certainty, I would rebrand in 2018 to Organista Home at some point. I started working with various coaches trying to move that idea forward even if I had no clue how. Releasing the fear of moving forward with it also released the block and clients were flying in! We were doing larger projects, staying true to our roots, and really taking care of our clients, like we had always done. Our reputation kept growing. When people heard about my organization company, they wanted to know more. We even partnered with a senior assisted living community and now had the great fortune to help the elderly with kid gloves and kindness and attention they deserved. We had won "Best Professional Organizer" for the third year in a row. I was featured on a few podcasts, and I was so ready to officially rebrand. While the coaches I worked with were supportive, for some reason I could not just get it off the ground.

But then another opportunity presented itself at the end of the summer. My friend Jenn was moving after almost a decade of being in her home. She had two kids, a family business, and no time to figure out how to pack all the stuff they'd accumulated over the years. I knew I could help her without a doubt. This was my wheelhouse. And as timing should have it, I had 3 weeks without clients. That was the exact time leading up to her move. Now why this is important, not only could I help a dear friend, but I knew she could and would return the favor. Jenn had experience building businesses. She was a coach, and even helped companies grow, expand, and create training materials. I knew she had a lot on her plate, but if I could help take moving off of it, maybe she could help me get Organista Home off the ground.

So one day I casually mentioned helping her move. She of course said it was too much for me to just do it as a favor. So the barter exchange was discussed. I was all in helping her every day release, repurpose, rehome, and recycle. She was packed up and ready to go, completely refreshed from the process, too!!

Jenn saw firsthand what my company did, and she was hooked, a believer for sure!

But again, my fear started to come into play. I knew she owed me some coaching sessions, but I found every excuse not to begin them. She mentioned it many times, but I kept myself busy. Finally, she drew a line in the sand, and at the end of that year a dear friend she said to me that it was time to launch Organista Home. Closing out the year in our highest financial year. And finally, I felt completely ready.

Ready, but still wondering how in the world I would be able to do that. Every time I thought about it in the several years since the idea came to me, I had thought and thought about it. There were so many things I would have to do, beyond my capabilities, or so I thought. How would I ever or could ever make a policies and procedures manual? I mean that was like impossible, almost like me going into space, impossible. Jenn was not worried, like she needed me to help her move, I needed her to help me grow. She knew my expertise, and this was hers. I trusted her. I was jumping, leaping, going for it!!

Funny enough at our very first official session, Jenn has recruiting new employees, and by week 2 I had switched over my website, my Facebook page, and announced that on January 1st our new name would be Organista Home! Over the next few weeks, Jenn helped me to create manuals, systems, firms, and trainings. She encouraged me to change my rate structure and clarify my offerings even more. She knew my worth. She knew the value my company brought to so many lives. I couldn't believe how it all started to come together. And I'm happy to report things are going beyond amazing. I've done things I never thought I could ever do. I have certified, bonded, insured employees with a policies and procedure manual. Business is great. Our new clients are paying our new rates, and we just finished up one of our largest 3-person jobs yet. 235 clients and we are still rocking, reaching the people that need us! And the donations have helped so many families in need.

Organista Home is expected to hit the 6-figure mark. Helping and supporting all those around us. Who would have thought just 8 years ago I'd be able to say that? Not me! Even 5 years ago when my business coach at the time asked what I'd like to make and feel comfortable with, I never dreamed this big! The pod idea is coming together and soon you will see Organista Home in cities around the country, and that is just the beginning. So, girl, just do it! You gotta grab those horns and get on it. Never let go. I believe in your gifts, your talents, and your ability to help others. Don't let hard times, rejections, or anything stop you. Begin now and dream big!

Make It Your Business to Not Let Heartbreak Break You and Build That Empire

Pick Up that Phone

Reach out to people. No risk, no reward, right? Snafus are part of the process, so you have to roll the dice, make connections, and see where it goes. You never know where that one phone call can take you, even if it just catapults you into believing more in yourself!

Aim to Fail More

Say what?! Aim to fail more? Heck yeah, it shows that you are putting yourself out there and trying!! Success can't happen in a test tube. You have to put yourself in real world situations where failure is just part of the deal! Learn the lessons you need to learn, but remember the lesson is never intended to shrink us. The lesson should never feed our ego. The lesson is there to help us grow and make us stronger.

Get Smarter Every Time

With every experience, you gain knowledge and wisdom. You learn to ask better questions. You learn to do your research and due diligence. And you learn the value of your village. Partner with people who have strengths in areas where you have less experience. Add value to others lives with your knowledge. You will see how much working smarter not harder will completely open up your world!

Know You are Worth It

Your dreams are worth every ounce of your being. You have to keep getting back in the saddle, even if it's easier to saddle up on the couch with some ice cream! Fear can be debilitating but it blocks all the goodness, the flow of energy, even abundance (boy that is still hard to learn!!). When you know you are worth it, keep moving forward, and claim your value, other people jump on board with you and can't help but know your worth too.

Section 3

Helping Others and Healing Ourselves

"I had no business helping other people pull their lives together, mine was still coming apart...but I dove right in and did it anyway."

CHAPTER
Eight

A Ticket to the Stars

"If you're offered a seat on a rocket ship, don't ask what seat. Just get on." ~ Sheryl Sandburg

So what would you say to a man that you respect, admire and have gone to church with for years, when he asks you to partner with him on a tent project to help the people of Haiti after the devastating earthquake in 2010?

I said, "Of course, why not?"

I had just finished up a massive collection for an orphanage in Dominican Republic where a lot of the Haitian orphans were sent afterwards. My friend Rosie's mother lived there and worked as a lawyer in the DR, so we had a direct connection and an urgent cry for help. She focused on collecting monetary donations for the shipping container we would need to use, and I focused on clothes, shoes, and toys that were to be sent in the container.

It's funny because whenever somebody has a need, I don't think twice I just jump in and call in the troops to help. I mean most people are happy to help! Why not say yes to the opportunity to help another person? One day that person in need could be you. I know it's been me a few times in my life! Oh, how I loved the photos that came back—absolutely priceless. And yes, the whole process was documented.

So back to Don and this tent idea. Don works in New York City in importing and exporting from what I know. So Don, being a very spiritual man felt compelled to do something to help after that earthquake.

Now a little story about Don and his unwavering faith and dedication to helping others. His mother went to a church that was being built in Korea. They were in need of money, so they were fundraising. Don's mother pledged 5 $10,000 plaques in each of her family member's names. Essentially thousands of people would be praying for Don and his family since those plaques would be prominently displayed in the church, and the $50,000 pledge would really help the church's mission. Of course, Don had no idea where he would get the $50k to pay for these plaques, but he had such strong faith, he knew the money would come. And Don was right, it did.

A Project with Purpose

Don impressed me with his kind, gentle way, and of course, his faith was inspiring. Don had resources in other countries and was doing research on making cost-effective tents that would be durable and would house families that needed shelter.

He made a contact and this company could make durable tents and attach a "Tents for Haiti" logo on them. These tents would cost $15 shipped! Sounds like a no-brainer, so we got to work. We created a website, and we started speaking at masses, collecting monetary donations, sold bulk clothing to increase proceeds! We even were written up in the paper, with an article featuring Don and me and the "Tents for Haiti" mission. The youth group jumped in, helping sell items, talking at masses at various churches, collecting donations. We spread the word the best we could and as often as we could.

Don and I were able to collect a good bit of money in which we gave to our church to now donate to our sister parish in Haiti. We felt good, we got the community involved and being as far as we were away from Haiti, we did the best we could. But, you see, after lots and lots of research, we realized the tents were just not going to work at all. Resourceful as he is and never wasteful, Father Bill sent the money to our sister parish in the mountains of Bainet which was completely leveled from the earthquake. To us, it didn't matter where the money went as long as we were doing good and the money was actually used to help others.

I'm so grateful that Don asked me to be a part of the Haiti project, not knowing what would come of it. I had never helped so many people so far away before, and it felt pretty darn good to know that after losing everything, people were given something to shelter them from the elements.

Listen, you don't have to know how to do something, you don't even have to know all of the "what." You just have to be open to incredible experiences that help others. When you just say yes, you learn whatever you need to learn along the way. You know, like that great quote from Ray Bradbury, "You've got to jump off a cliff and build your wings on the way down."

Taking Jumping to a Whole New Level

So growing up I kind of prided myself on being a bit of a goody two-shoes. I followed the rules to a tee, and the riskiest thing I did was scour the house for loose change so I could have enough money to get myself a Carvel ice cream sundae without my mom knowing. Ooh, what a rule breaker I was!

When I got into my teens, the boys did have an effect on me. The next thing you know I was sixteen and taking my mom's car out while they were asleep. I'd pick up my friends and we'd meet up with the cute guys we we're friends with. I was clever though. We had a real cow bell at the front door that would clang when anyone walked into the house. I would stuff that bell so full of toilet paper just so I wouldn't get caught! The only one who caught wind was our softball coach. He somehow overheard my friend and me talking about our escapades and boy was he mad! He never worked us so hard. Plus my mom wasn't super strict.

One morning I actually came in at daybreak, and she was standing there tapping her foot. She was so mad, she put me up against a wall and here I was, acting all innocent telling her

I just went to Dunkin' Donuts, and eventually the whole thing just kind of blew over.

But that taste of breaking the rules sent a rush right through me. It was exhilarating really. And as I got older, I realized I didn't always have to be the goody two-shoes. So I took a few more risks and broke a few more rules, and all in all was just living and learning. After my marriage crumbled, though, boy did I just want to dive into helping people. Little did I know my risk-taking self would emerge again soon, but in a whole new way.

Several months after our big Tents for Haiti drive ended, Vee from our church presented us with an opportunity. She was one of the direct connections to Haiti. Vee was born in Haiti, grew up there, and then moved to Asbury Park. She became a nurse right here at Jersey Shore Hosptial for many, many years. Vee was still going back to Haiti often and knew Father Maxis down there. So when it was time for her to go back to visit and for one of the biggest festivals of Saint Jacque, she suggested that Don and I should join her since we spent so much time working on behalf of the people of her home country.

Me?

Little old me leave the country on my own?

I had never been so far away. Plus going to Haiti meant leaving my children to go visit complete strangers with medical supplies and see what the money we raised had built. I mean, my family helped people, but they never would even leave the state let alone the country! Nope, this was nothing that anyone in my direct family had ever done. But I guess my sixteen-year-old, risk-taking skills came in handy paired with my goody two-shoes inner child who still loved helping people. Perfect match.

What was I to do but of course say yes?

Why not?

I mean what an opportunity it would be. So July of 2011 Don, Vee, and I were heading to Newark Airport to fly to Port-au-Prince. I had really no idea what I was doing but I knew everything would work out and be absolutely amazing! I mean who gets to really go to Haiti and I'm not talking about Labadee, the section owned by Royal Caribbean Cruise Ships. I was going into the city and the remote mountains with no running water, no electricity. At that time my biggest concern was what was I going to eat, being the picky childlike eater I was. I handled that, no problem. My solution was to just pack trail mix bars.

So we landed, but my suitcase did not; it was to arrive the next day. I was fine with that, it was all so exciting! From the airport, we were immediately thrown into the bustling town of Port Au Prince. Thankfully and of course gratefully we had Vee with us. She knew the ins and outs of everything. She guided us through the airport and into our transport. On our drive to the hostel, we saw Haiti full-on—dumpsters of trash in the streets burning the garbage, crazy rigged contraptions of cars that would squeeze 15 people inside, two wheeled vehicles and their drivers without helmets and too many passengers, no street lights, massive damage, wreckage everywhere, and loads of makeshift housing, not to mention pigs and cows roaming everywhere. Sensory overload.

Just Beyond Incredible

We arrived at the hostel and came through the gate to see an armed guard with a very large gun right before the entrance. Here we were, staying in a Catholic hostel run by a little nun who had lived there for years. She'd assured us Haiti was absolutely safe. Not to question a woman of the cloth, but I wondered if she was telling the truth, I mean the gun made my antennas go up for sure. She collected our passports and kept them in a lockbox. The lockbox held quite a few passports for all the missionaries staying there. It was way more than I anticipated. So we walked around and looked for an unclaimed bed. Vee and I stayed in one room and Don opted for the screened in section on the roof so he could sleep under the stars.

That night Don and I sat up late just looking up at the sky. I have never in my life felt closer to the Milky Way, as if I could just reach out and grab a star; almost like I could walk right up to the moon if I just had a ladder. Was I dreaming? I mean sneaking out at all hours of the night with my mom's car was nothing compared to this. I never even looked up at the sky back then. Here I was, halfway around the world, but all of a sudden the world was just so small.

And almost like I stepped back in time.

I mean, the food in the part of Haiti we were in was really only the food that grew locally. There were no 7-11s or fast food restaurants there. But that even turned out to be a huge blessing. Sometime before our Haiti trip Don had a heart attack. He knew something wasn't right, and so he went to the hospital and shared his symptoms with the staff. They quickly knew it was serious and tried to rush him in right away. The emergency room was very busy at that time, so Don, being the humble, kind man he was, refused to be pushed ahead of any others that were waiting. He felt if they were in the ER, each of their emergencies were just as critical as his. He believed so strongly that God would take care of him, he didn't need or want to skip the line. Well Don was right. He did survive the heart attack, thankfully, and shortly after we were sitting on the rooftop in Haiti.

And what better place to find food after you've had a heart attack? I mean food was fresh and healthy. Don's staples on the trip were the coconut water that fell right from the coconut trees and opened quickly with a slice of the machete and the endless amounts of fresh fruit. He needed to reset his heart, and it turned out that Haiti was just the place to do it.

The next morning the town was buzzing. And by morning, I mean WAY before my normal morning. At home this was still prime sleeping time to me. But in Haiti, it is a common practice to get up super early before the sun is in full effect because it gets so very hot during the day. So it was like 6 am, no joke, and we were on the roof again, watching a soccer game in the field next to us. It was wild. Almost like a dream, and I just felt in awe and so grateful the whole time. If I hadn't said yes, I would have never experienced any of this.

Was I in a 3rd world country?

Yes.

Was I in a guarded hostel?

Sure.

But the people, the community, the land, the sky, the coconut trees…these are some of the things dreams are made of. My friend that has traveled the world extensively, once told me she would go almost anywhere, but has not gone to Haiti. She still can't believe I did.

So on day 2, after thankfully finding my bag at the airport, we were about to embark on our next journey to see where the money we raised went. A 6-hour drive up hills, through mountains, around treacherous terrain, with no guardrails, no street lights, all in a car very different than the ones we have in the States. That drive nearly did me in in both good ways and not so pleasant ones. I mean, whether it was the 2 flat tires, the bulldozing of the mountain, the teeny tiny car lanes, or the steep, very steep drops, or watching the glorious sun as it set, looking out at the beautiful greenery—I just took it all in.

Well guess what? We made it safely. Don and I got the full tour of the grounds which were small. The money we had raised built a two-room structure and the foundation of a school. We were visiting during one of the holiest festivals of the year and the people of the church gave us the two rooms to sleep in. Don on one side and Vee, Paula (a resident of Haiti and New Jersey), and me on the other. I even saved the handwritten welcome note that was on the pillow. Again, like another world, everything just touched my heart so much. Well, I guess not everything. I mean, don't ask me about the pail in the corner that let's just say I never used. There are some things I am grateful we have at home, like working toilets. Call me spoiled, but that was something I could not get used to.

So during this festival, the most holy members of the church traveled to where we were, and they had given up the only true structure they had to let us sleep there. They treated us like royalty. All the other visitors slept in tents on the gravel and did so happily. And these visitors said they would never ever forget us. I mean like everyone that crossed our path said this. They were so grateful that we went to visit them. I didn't completely understand why they would be so grateful to us. We were no different. If anything, they were the ones to be admired. The people were kind, caring, and did whatever they could to make us feel at home, even if we did not speak the same language. Did I mention there were just 2 people that spoke English?

The hills and mountain tops were simply incredible. The pictures are captured truly in my heart because the actual photos I do have do not do them justice. The mountains were absolutely nothing like the city. On our walks, we would see people traveling carrying water, in buckets. That looked hard and like it took a ton of balance. We would see these little homes, huts really, and I suppose the lucky ones had a solar panel for their phone lines. Everyone smiled, people even with very little modern-day conveniences, seemed genuine and happy. The air was so pure up there. There were many above the ground caskets and tombs—I suppose for the very fortunate people. I remember thinking to myself what a beautiful place for your body to be.

While up there on top of the world in Haiti, Don and I came up with dozens of ideas to help the economy. Maybe one day.

As we left after spending 3 days there, I couldn't help but think of the differences from the American way of life. I mean, life was centered around church to the Haitians. The masses, which we attended, often were hours long, and there were not even seats for all the people who attended! So think about it. When the people walked to mass, and some come from as far as 2 hours away, they carry their chairs with them upside down on the top of their head!! And they are literally walking for miles (because cars are so rare and a luxury), also holding their hanging clothes enclosed in plastic, so when they arrive they can change in the woods and be "fresh" for church. So they are walking for miles, carrying chairs, clothes, food, and even babies to attend a mass on a concrete slab with no walls or ceiling unless you count the recycled cell phone plastic marketing piece they used as tarps. I'm telling you, talk about perspective.

I learned so much in those 5 days about life, faith, joy, blessings, and what truly matters. I know I was meant to go to Haiti, and while the people there were grateful to us, it was us who really benefitted from that trip. Life changing 10000%. It just solidified that I had a purpose here, that joy doesn't come from circumstances or the number of bedrooms in your home, that the pure beauty of God's creation blows away any man-made interior design, and that there is nothing better than using our time in service of others.

If I was a nervous nelly, if I listened to naysayers, I would have missed all of this. So I am telling you, make it your business to say YES to experiences that would normally frighten the heck out of you. You will not be the same afterward!

Make It Your Business to Say YES to Unique Opportunities

Get that Passport

You never know when you're going to need it, and it's always good to have! Getting a passport is like making a promise to yourself that you are going to use it! Traveling provides us so many incredible opportunities, so don't hesitate to fill out the paperwork and take that passport photo!

Don't Overthink It

When we spend too much time weighing pros and cons, asking everyone and anyone their opinion, or worrying about what ifs, we clearly miss out on the awesome things that are in store. Don't Google it, go for it!!

Say Yes to Kind, Like-Minded People

When someone presents an opportunity to you, and they are in alignment with who you are, that should be enough. Just say YES to unique opportunities and let life show you how it's done!

Get Involved

Think you have no unique opportunities coming to you? Think again! Opportunities are EVERYWHERE!! You just have to get involved with causes you care about and put yourself out there. You don't need a lot of time to volunteer. Literally the time you take scrolling social media can be used in a soup kitchen or collecting clothes for people in need. It can be just an hour a month, but in that hour your opportunity can come in the blink of an eye.

CHAPTER
Nine

The Sisters God Gave Me

"I love when people that have been through hell walk out of the flames carrying buckets of water for those still consumed by the fire..."
~ Stephanie Sparkles

When I was about six years old, my godmother took me and my siblings to a park. She took pictures and my smile was literally ear to ear. I threw my hands in the air, jumped, and smiled wide. I looked oh so happy. It's crazy because I became self-conscious of my smile as I got older and my teeth didn't come in as straight as the magazines said they should. I mastered the art of the closed mouth smile, let me tell you.

The truth is that photo of six-year-old me was carefree and light. If you flip through albums, year after year I seemed to be carrying more and more weight on my shoulders and it showed in my eyes. It showed in my facial expressions, even if I was smiling, there was a bit of sadness still present behind the grin. Understandable, I know. I was a young mom, struggling financially, trying to find my way in the world, in a less than stable relationship most of the time. But I swear, my girlfriends gave me back my life. And I have a photo to prove it.

Yep.

A photo from my 35th birthday where I had my first annual birthday celebration. I threw my hands in the air, jumped, and smiled wide. I hadn't even realized the similarity of those photos until recently. My girlfriends gave me air when I felt like I was suffocating. And that's why this chapter means so very much to me. Supportive women helped me to get me to this point in my life. I count on my friends for so much. Some friends have seen me at very different, extremely difficult times and they held me up, shined their light on me, and wouldn't let me forget that I was special. These women helped me to continue to see all that was inside of me when I couldn't get out of my own way. Times were tough and not easy—oh how I wanted the white picket fence lifestyle you see in old movies. But my life was so very different from that. It was not all roses, rainbows, and sunshine. I had to handle some real crap, some of my own making and some just from the hand I was dealt. Sure I do have this tough exterior but on the inside, I was still that six-year-old girl who just wanted love. So many things cut me to my core, especially when it came to finances.

And who was always there, cheering me on or lending a buck, or making me feel safe?

The incredible women I get to call my girlfriends. I knew that whatever came my way, I always had someone I could call who'd listen to me (or I will listen to them of course) or vent with or to make me laugh. At some point I released the worry that came with not having enough money to pay the rent. I just let that shit go because I knew with so many friends, we would never be homeless. I have at least a few friends who would take the kids and me in if it came to that, and of course I would do the same for them.

You might be wondering how I could be so sure that we'd have a place to go if push came to shove. Let me tell you, I've seen my dear friends do this firsthand with others. At the time, I was even more fascinated by the fact that my friends didn't even charge them a penny to stay with them. Now you may be thinking, "No duh, Jess, that's what friends just do!" But it was such a foreign concept to me, since I had in fact paid rent since my late teens and that was to live with my parents. I didn't completely understand or find it fair, but that was the way it was and that was okay.

Having solid friendships like this gave me incredible peace of mind. So knowing we would never be homeless really helped when I finally was ready to release that stress. With child support nearly nonexistent, times got tough. I mean really tough at certain points. But I knew my friends would have my back to the best of their abilities as I would theirs. Whatever I could do, I mean I have offered out my basement and my couch several times to close friends and their families.

Assistance Without Shame

When I was working for the church, I was having a tough time keeping up with the utilities. Sometimes, I just had to pay rent first and foremost to keep a roof over our heads, everything else was secondary. St. Vincent De Paul Society has a chapter in my church, and they set meeting dates to see walk-ins. Anyone is welcome to go and seek assistance. You share your hardships and your bills or whatever it might be, and they do what they can for you. I didn't even know this was a thing until I needed it myself. Sure they have those little boxes in the back of the church that stated in brass "St. Vincent De Paul," but damned if I knew what that meant! As I kid I can remember shoving a few coins in the box, not ever really knowing what that was other than assuming it had to be something for the poor people.

So fast forward, and all of the sudden I am one of those poor people. Here I am in the basement, and I'm going in there, and I'm going to ask for help. Earlier that day, I had spoken with my friend Frankie who was on the volunteer committee for the organization. I broke down and told her I was going, as ashamed as I was it had to be done. There was just a small window of time that they would see people, and that time was passing me by because I couldn't bring myself out of the communal ladies' room to go into the room. I thought all the thoughts . . .

I don't need it as bad as others.

I'll be fine.

Things would work out.

It wasn't that bad.

My heart and head couldn't take much more. I was spinning. Then wouldn't you know Frankie walks in and says, "Where have you been? What's going on, we have been waiting for you?"

That is when I proceeded to tell her all the statements I had been telling myself. She insisted I was crazy and convinced me to go! Finally, with some hesitation, I followed. I went into the all-white classroom and there sat half a dozen various church members that I either knew or had seen around.

That's when they opened. A very kind woman began and stated that this was a place of love and there was no room for embarrassment or shame. She explained that people went through rough times and that was all this was, a place to get some assistance. What a calming relief I had immediately felt. All the people I had helped throughout my many years in various ways, now I knew how important it was to make them feel as if we are all one. It was beautiful, and I will never forget that moment or Frankie, my dear friend. Then they said a little prayer and they were able to help me and my family. In such a kind and generous way, never making me feel anything but loved. This profound experience showed me that we are all deserving of assistance without shame. I'm so grateful for that experience, and that I was on the receiving end. We all deserve help for bumps in the road. You get what you give.

Friendships Made in the Basement

One of my other responsibilities while working at the church was helping run the after-school program with Sister Kate and Antonia. This program took place in the very large spacious basement of the church. Now, Asbury Park has seen its ups and downs. It is a small city nestled along the coast of the Jersey Shore, most known for Bruce Springsteen and the Stone Pony. Now back in the heyday of Asbury Park, they actually held masses down in the church basement as well. Then the turbulent times of Asbury Park happened. The race riots destroyed the town, poverty became the norm. Sadly, loads and loads of people left seemingly for good, well not until now that it's on the up and up again.

When I was first starting out at the church, Antonia and I both working part-time, we had to get the basement ready for the after-school program. There were several classrooms down there, all new and just beautiful. During school hours it was used for ESL run by Brother James and volunteers. Then, in the evening it was used for religious education. A thriving community center for the 3 different communities that were now together from the diocese and local churches in disrepair. We held American, Haitian, and Spanish communities, such a beautiful melting pot that worked so nicely together.

So Antonia and I would clean and prep those closets, storage areas, offices, and bathrooms for all these children to come for free and attend the after-school program. There was also a free summer camp program held there. Sister Kate would have the youth group members essentially be in charge of the summer camp, and we were there to oversee it. I didn't quite understand or completely agree with this format, but in hindsight I began to see how these older teenagers were learning leadership and how to handle all the different facets of this camp. Giving them skills most teens would never experience! They created schedules, class trips, and events.

It was in that very basement I met some very dear friends that I'm forever grateful for. Antonia is an incredibly strong women raising 4 beautiful daughters essentially by herself. Her daughters were given the very best education Antonia could provide for them through Sister's Academy, an all-girls charter school in Asbury Park and then all 4 attended Red Bank Catholic. These girls were raised to cook, clean, volunteer, and work hard long before they even understood it. Antonia's daughters practically lived in that church basement and never complained, and trust me, they were there a whole lot. Antonia would clean homes all day and then head right over to the basement to start her work there.

After working together for a few months, Antonia had shared with me that she had never given her oldest daughter Jessica a Quinceañera, and Jessica was about to turn 18! Well before you know it, I was all in, dove deep right in to helping Antonia give Jessica a truly special 18th birthday party. I did whatever I could to make this huge event happen.

The one job that I will never forget is hanging gold and cranberry streamers from the tall ceiling in the church basement where the party would take place, in the large middle room. I hung literally close to 500 4-foot-long streamers over the dance floor. The Rojas girls practically lived in the church basement volunteering their time, whether they liked it or not. So I wanted to do something to make the church basement not feel like the church basement, but rather transform it into the most beautiful space to honor them. So providing this fun dance floor effect was what I chose to give to her. Never comfortable on ladders, let alone looking up while reaching up, it was a challenge and a total doozy, but it came out perfect— time and effort well spent! Antonia and these girls had given so much to others and this was their turn to receive back.

Then there was Tami, a very kind mother of 9. I met Tami and her crew when their church had merged with ours. Her family consisted of 9 beautiful children. 5 girls and 4 boys. They would be in mass every Sunday filling up an entire pew of just them—what an amazing sight to see. They would be sitting in the first section of pews right at the front on the right side. My family would traditionally sit midsection on the left side. I would sit in mass in awe behind them and try and count how many there were. On a few occasions we might exchange a word or two. I remember going up to Phil, Tami's oldest son, in the basement one time for some type of coffee club connection and saying hello. I asked him just how many brothers and sisters he had. He politely answered he was 1 of 9. Wow, just wow!

At that time, I would go to the local Shoprite for groceries. I realized Tami's husband, Phil Sr., worked security for the police department there in the evenings. With 9 children, I mean I'm sure a family would need to take any overtime they could possibly get! One day I was in line at the deli and a woman next to me placed her order at the counter. I thought I was hearing things as she said, "4 lbs. of cheese and 4 lbs. of ham." I looked up thinking, holy Toledo, that's a lot of lunch meat. I lifted my eyes from my long to-do list, and noticed it was Tami. I had barely known her at the time, and so I said a quick hello and mentioned something about the 4 lbs. and laughed. You could immediately feel her kind, friendly energy. It was a brief interaction but a nice one.

I had met Tami and her husband sometime prior in the basement of Holy Spirit Church. I know lots of things happen in that church. In order to work for the Catholic church it was required that you get a background check and take Virtus training. (VIRTUS is a program created by the National Catholic Risk Retention Group in the United States with a "Protecting God's Children" component that combats sexual abuse of children in the church. It is currently in use in over 80 dioceses in the United States.) So we spent several hours together as Phil and Tami were both the teachers. At that time, the two of them were running religious education for the Missionaries of Charity. That group included close to 100 of children from low income areas. It was a massive undertaking, and there was a huge language barrier since most of the parents and a good portion of the children only spoke Spanish. Talk about being selfless, every single Saturday they volunteered teaching this class for hours!!

Tami was very involved in her former parish in Neptune.

That church was structurally condemned, and so the parish members moved to Holy Spirit. So when Tami's kids started to attend our free summer camp she would do the pickups and drop offs. She always came in smiling, sweet, and nice. It was a pleasure to see her come in, and her children were terrific in all senses of the word. The older ones were in youth group running the day to day operations and her younger children attended the camp. The camp was a lot of work and I can't say it was action-packed but once again no complaints. They were just good.

Then during the school year, Tami organized her new job which meant combining and running the two religious education programs—talk about an enormous task! Almost doubling her students and only running one day after school and one on Saturdays.

So now Tami was becoming a staple in the basement as well. And lucky for us! What a bright light and spirit. It was there in the basement one day, that Tami shared with me what was going on in her home life, and it was a shocker. The devastating diagnosis of cancer topped with the infidelity of her husband. Words came out of her mouth that I just wasn't ready for, from the outside they were peaches 'n cream, so I just could not believe it all. At the time she had confided in me, I didn't feel that we were that close per say; we were friendly, but this was deep, deep stuff. I was blown away and honored that she trusted me enough to begin to share what was really going on in her life—a side that obviously no one really knew about. The Siedle family was the poster child for

beautiful Catholic families. I wasn't sure what to do, what to say. So I chose to just hold space for her and listen. After that conversation we just grew to be closer and closer.

Sunshine, Rain, and
One of the Worst Phone Calls of My Life

We had great times together personally and professionally. We became such good friends, anytime I had any type of event or celebration, I could always count Tami in. I mean, dinner dances, movie nights, birthday celebrations, workshops, out of state conferences…I'd never have to ask Tami twice. She was so happy to be out doing whatever, as long as we were together, it really didn't matter. She'd laugh, talk, joke, dance, and even hula hoop close to midnight. Tami exuded kindness and fun. She was pure sunshine to be around. For the unfortunate things she was going through, she never complained about it or showed any weakness. She was in the midst of a divorce at that time and although she didn't share everything with me, I knew things weren't right in regard to Phil. I knew he had to be abusive in some way, mentally or physically, maybe both. They sought counseling, but it didn't help. The actions continued and she was ready to close that chapter as hard as it was.

So we enjoyed the times we had together in the church and outside of it. We partnered on many projects. We worked hard and ultimately it was always to help others. We just got what was truly important, and we did it kind of like Laverne and Shirley. I'll never forget after one of my big birthday gatherings, Tami had given me a gift. I opened the box and found this beautiful silver and multi rose quartz stone bracelet. Oh, it was so beautiful. Tami had recently learned about the significance of rose quartz. She had rose quartz stones all over her office, so it didn't surprise me of all the stones to pick from she would pick this small pink round rose quartz stone. On the end of this bracelet there was an engraving and it read, "Jess & Tami" and on the reverse side it said, "God made us sisters." I still carry it around on important days in my life, even with the broken clasp. Knowing whenever I had anything important, Tami would be there, so I keep it to know she is, even while I write this difficult story.

When the after-school program moved locations to Our Lady of Mount Carmel School, the principal Sister Jude asked if I could help her organize her office. The next thing you know, I wound up working for that school part-time as well. One of my jobs was to write postcards to the parents of the children that were "stars of the week." I did this for a few years and at that time Tami's younger children were attending that school. Literally, there was not a week that went by that I wasn't sending a card home for one of Tami's children. Dorothy, Maria, and Stephen were kind to their classmates, did all their homework, got good test grades, respected their teachers and peers. These kids did it all and in the best ways possible.

On June 16, 2015, I got a call after my kids left for school from my friend Lesly. Her calling me midday was totally normal, but what she said on this day was anything but. It was on this phone call that she shared with me Tami was shot and died. Her ex-husband Phil had killed her.

I didn't believe it.

He didn't kill her.

He couldn't kill her.

Lesly was wrong.

Tami was fine.

There was a mix-up. If Phil killed anyone it would have to be his girlfriend, the woman he had the affair with. It couldn't be true. Just the previous weekend we were all together celebrating Kirsten and Phillip's college graduation. Dancing, eating under tents in Tami's back yard. Her daughter Teresa had slept over at my house that night—the first time she had ever had a sleepover. I took her to Jimmy's in Asbury to celebrate with my daughter Reilly. All the photos I took at the party and then at dinner, showing happiness, laughter, and smiles. We all had such an amazing time.

How could it be?

At some point I finally believed Lesly. The shooting went right to social media because there were people on the streets filming the whole thing. I won't go into details, and I can say I have never watched one second of that filming because there was no reason to watch. Why would I ever want to see it?

Oh my heart broke in two that day. I lost my soul sister. I beat myself up, wondering if I could have done more. I wished I could have protected her. I didn't know Phil was that dangerous. According to everyone who did know that, it wouldn't have mattered. It didn't do Tami's children any good to have me questioning myself. I had to move forward and do whatever I could to help her family, the way I know she would help mine.

When that happened, I wasn't extremely close to the children. It was mainly Tami and me doing things together. Of course I knew them all, but my friendship was with Tami. So I didn't even have all the kids' numbers. I tried reaching out via FB anything to get ahold of them. I remember driving over to the house and leaving a note on the door for someone to call me.

Tami was very close with Frankie, who also was very involved in the church. You may recall Frankie and I worked together, and her children had attended the youth group summer camp. I called Frankie, and she connected me with Tami's children. So many people were trying to help Tami's family, so many friends and strangers doing all types of things, but there was no rhyme or reason. So I pulled on my organizational skills and suggested we start a Facebook page dedicated to helping the kids. I did this with Kirsten and Phillip's consent. I came up with the name Tami's Legacies and we moved forward. It grew and grew. We created a dinner program that lasted months and months long. There were so many complete strangers doing what they could to help. We had significant milestones that the kids were hitting, like a sweet sixteen and graduation, not to mention holiday's and birthdays, so with the communities help I was able to arrange multiple events for them. I've never seen anything more beautiful. Complete strangers helping in so many ways.

Through Tami's Legacies on Facebook, I spread the word about what was needed and updates about the family. Maria's 13th birthday would be coming up. What a milestone for a lovely young lady, so I thought of throwing her a birthday party and I asked the community to help. Maria had a beautiful pool party in the summer to celebrate her big day. The party was held at a woman named Kirsten's home, she is a friend of mine and opened her back yard for this special day. My girlfriend Joanna made Maria custom soccer blue and green sugar cookie favors, plus all the food, drinks, and games were donated from various people and businesses in the community. A band even played. Complete strangers showed up to drop off goods for this very special girl. It was simply amazing. Then there was Dorothy who was going to turn 16, so many thanks to Alissa of The Renaissance in Ocean Township that gave us the most incredible deal to throw Dorothy the Halloween themed party of her dreams. Makeup and hair services were donated, the candy bar, the DJ, all given with no strings attached. People went above and beyond to come through for this event.

There was Monica's pre prom event, Teresa's Fun Time America party, birthday card club, Christmas collections, Easter baskets, and a food chain that literally went on for months. Complete strangers, friends, and family all pulling together to help love and support these children.

Since that time, I have also grown much closer to the children having them over, celebrating and checking in. They are all so incredible and I cherish the time that I do have with them. It's like I am with Tami, just in different versions. It takes a village to raise children and if something happened to me, I would only hope the village would do the same for my children. I could never write a chapter on friendship without telling you about my dear Tami. And I wish I had something more profound to say about this horrific end to Tami's life here on Earth. I only know that her light is still shining bright through each of her extraordinary children, and through every life she has ever touched, and that list is long!

Make it Your Business to Be Helpful and Kind to Everyone, As You Don't Know What's Going On Behind Closed Doors

Smile at Strangers

It's a small thing with a huge impact. Smiling can make a world of difference for someone going through a tough time. That connection can open doors to conversations and real friendships can come through. Who knew Tami smiling at the deli counter and a laugh over ham and cheese would lead to such a friendship?

Be Open and Receptive

Friendship comes in all shapes, sizes, colors, sexes, forms. Connect with people who don't always fit the mold of your usual friends. There is so much to learn from one another, that you never want to be closed off to the possibility of friendship.

Listen to Words Spoken and Unspoken

When you really listen to people, you can hear what they are not saying and provide comfort just with your presence. Sometimes all we need is to feel heard, and that space creates the best kind of friendships.

Show Appreciation

The smallest of gestures can show a friend you care, and that you are there for her. Bake a tray of brownies, send a handwritten note, talk her off the ledge when she's locked herself in the bathroom. You get what I mean! Show your friends you care regularly, and you'll be amazed at how deep the friendship can grow.

CHAPTER
Ten

When It's Time to Rise

"The success of every woman should be the inspiration to another. We should raise each other up. Make sure you're very strong, be extremely kind, and above all, be humble."
~ Serena Williams

So a few years back, I had this crazy idea that people would love to hear my organizational tales. I mean whenever sharing what I did in a room full of people, most people asked a bunch of questions and wanted to know more. From hoarding horror stories to the everyday, people wanted to know more from the only organizer in the room. So one day I thought I should write a book about it—not disclosing my clients names of course, but just some of the tales. I had so many! The problem was that I did not think of myself as a gifted writer in any sense by any means, especially all those years ago. So my dear friend Natalie, who has a knack for words, popped into my head. I thought that maybe she would like to assist me in writing the book—the content would be mine based on my experiences, kind of like a fly on the wall type of look. Pretty good, right? I know I mean I can't even tell you how many times I get, "Have you ever worked with a Hoarder?" and "What was the craziest thing that you have seen?"

I had it all planned out, how I would ask Natalie to jump in on this with me. It felt like I was going to propose to her, it was that important. I had asked her to meet me one evening someplace convenient for her and she picked The Molly Pitcher, a beautiful hotel with restaurant and bar right on the water in the lovely vibrant town of Red Bank. I waited for her in the lobby. I'll never forget my palms were sweaty, my nerves were getting the best of me. She was a great friend, but would she agree to this crazy idea of mine?! I knew how much she loved writing and her popular blog MILF (Mother I'd Like to Friend) was always a hit.

She arrived and I popped the question right away. She was honored but would have to think about it. Natalie had 2 young children and knew that this would be a big commitment of time. But within a few days, Natalie got back to me saying she was in! So here I had an idea that I felt was too big for me to do alone, I reached out to a friend to help and she said YES! I was so excited, and soon after we were collaborating, doing research, and reaching out to anyone that might be able to offer guidance.

Social Connections and Putting It Out There

The great Stephanie Evanovich, a New York Times Best-Selling Author, just so happened to live in my small town of Wanamassa at that time. We were connected through social media. She went through the Ocean Township schools with my mother and uncles. So guess what? I just messaged her directly and asked her if we could pick her brain. I mean of course, why wouldn't this famous author meet with us, I mean come on really? She responded, and soon after Stephanie, Natalie, and I met in a small little luncheonette called Edies. Stephanie's vibrant personality filled up the entire small room, let me tell you. And it was the beginning of a friendship. I also pledged that one day when I'm a New York Times Best-Selling Author, I would make time for hopeful, aspiring authors to pick my brain, too. That meeting with Stephanie was so very helpful!

I still had questions, though. Even more popped up after meeting with Stephanie. So, you know I've never been embarrassed to ask for help and put out there what I needed. One day on Facebook, I had posted something about writing a book, and a friend commented that I should connect with Jennifer Tuma-Young, since she was a published author and from the same small town, Wanamassa. I looked her up and could see Jenn was an uberbusy woman in the book world. She was speaking at multiple events around the country and even on TV. Well Jenn got notified of her being tagged in my post and she private messaged little old me asking basically how could she help?

Are you freaking kidding me, how cool was that??

Soon after we set up a meeting, where Natalie and I found out we were doing the process essentially backwards. Jenn explained that she did the exact same thing as us and wanted to save us years of trying to figure out the crazy nonfiction book world!! She had received dozens of rejections before landing an incredible agent and eventually a crazy big book deal, so I totally trusted and valued her advice. I mean, it was a bit deflating to know we would have to change direction, but I was not defeated. Jenn's kindness and light just flowed through her. She gave us hope, and this would not be the last time you will hear about Jenn.

And look, between Natalie, Stephanie, and Jenn, I connected with them, and asked 3 big "favors." You know each and every one of these lovely women said yes without hesitation. If I can say anything to you, it is this, you've gotta reach out and ask! The women who helped me said that they too had reached out and asked people for help, and they wanted to pay it forward. I mean, Jenn connected with her agent because she asked a total stranger to pick his brain on the book world. The ripple is huge. Ask for help!!

Jenn and I stayed in contact and became instant friends. I remember sharing an overview of my story with her in the Staples parking lot. Don't ask me why we got into this deep conversation standing outside of our cars, but it was there. Somehow I began telling her about some of my challenges, my obstacles, my Haiti trip, and she listened intently—a true friend that was truly interested in me.

It was around the time Jenn was planning BOLDHER, a women's conference in a rural hotel built in 1840 in Stroudsmoor PA. I would see the updates of her awesome speakers, awesome sponsors, and the coolest location. Never thinking twice about it, other than good wishes for her of course, and thinking maybe one day I would be speaking and sharing my story at events like Jenn did. Well that day came way sooner than I imagined, because a few days after our Staples conversation, Jenn asked me if I might be interested in being on the panel at the end of this event. She said the panel was about women helping others, women who have been through a lot, but still found it in their hearts to be of service. She called me an inspiration. Say what?!?! Are you kidding me?? I mean who was I? And why? I was just like everyone else. I was no different, if anything I didn't think I had the credentials to be up on that panel. But Jenn somehow felt differently, and of course I said yes! I mean how hard could it be?

So Jenn and her business partner at the time offered complimentary rooms to the speakers, since it was out of state. It sounded like a dream. So I spread the word of BOLDHER and had about 10 of my good friends join me. This would be a commitment financially, logistically, and in time. Plus it would be like a little journey, taking all of us just about 2 hours away on a road trip. In one car we had Antonia, Frankie, Tami, Melissa, Jennifer and Reilly. We had a blast driving up there in my white minivan. Laughing and fooling around the entire time, cracking jokes. I had a van full of women that gave their all to just about everything to anyone in need. These women thought of others before themselves. That is one of the reasons this day was so special, no one in this van had an abundance of money and or time, but they chose to spend their day to support me. We would share 2 rooms in that lovely inn, making memories and even a captured video or two. These all became so special especially after Tami's passing.

The second car carpooled up with Nancy, Natalie and Beth. Once again choosing to support me, taking a full day off to be there for me. How could I be so lucky? Although they did not stay over, I heard the travel time talk was stellar giving them their own memories.

Photos beautifully capture the crew in front of the mountainous rock—a long line of kind, loving and supportive women. So ladies, I can't encourage you enough to take the day, support your friends, and invest in yourselves because it will come back to you in some way shape or form.

I got to see Jenn in action that day, and you could tell she wanted nothing more than the women in the room to feel loved and that they were capable of anything. She was wearing a simple maxi dress, side braid, and a starfish necklace. Something I would have picked. Nothing over the top. She showed up to serve the room not be the center of it. I later learned that about 20 of the attendees were women from a shelter. Jenn gave them free tickets, and she and her young daughter helped the women get ready for the event. While much of her time was spent on that, and of course the event itself, she didn't think twice about her own outfit, makeup, or hair. Jenn although she seemed so different with her travel and TV stuff was actually just like us, doing anything to help another.

Tami particularly liked Jenn's talk, and so I introduced her to Jenn afterwards. Tami pointed out that Jenn was wearing a starfish necklace, Tami's symbol for healing through her difficult divorce battle. Little did we know at the time that Tami's words healed Jenn, because Jenn was internally beating herself up for not spending time putting an outfit together. Later Jenn told me that she believed she was meant to wear that Starfish necklace, that God was her stylist that day, just so she could have that connection with Tami. Jenn even gave me the necklace after Tami's passing. It's crazy how this all came to be, looking back now. When I met Jenn to pick her brain, I had no clue what was yet to come for us.

Seeing a Need and Being Called to Fill It

Ever since I founded my company Organize By Design, I began to see a pattern. Women that lacked connection with other women but craving to do so. Women that needed a tribe. This really affected me. I was blessed since coming into myself in my early 30's surrounded by tons of women I called dear friends. I wanted to do something to help my clients as well, connect with other women of all types from all different backgrounds with all unique stories. My clients soon crossed over to friends. I would invite them to any event that I would throw or whenever I had the opportunity to bring someone to one. As I would host these parties, I started to see something beautiful. True connections. Each woman would find a friend or even a tribe and become close. I loved seeing on Facebook all the new friendships that were forming. What a blessing! Women stepping out of their comfort zone to attend something I had invited them to, promising them it would be great, and a lot of my clients took that leap. I'm still doing that to this day, including and inviting women to whatever I can, because I believe everyone deserves a circle. Bravo to the women that trust me and the women that join me, even if they are unsure!

Now you may recall a group I mentioned earlier in the book—WIP (Women in Power). At each meeting there would be a member spotlight and a canned good collection. These meetings really changed the game for me. I was still the quiet girl in the corner, sort of, but I took in every moment with this group. I saw how they supported each other in business with ideas, suggestions, giving business to one another. As I referenced before I had never been a part of anything like this before. There was so much respect, admiration, kindness, and true interest in each and every one of these women. Remember, it was at the end of this group's December meeting of 2010, when I began to find my voice when I asked the collective group, "Do you think there is a need for this home organizing thing?" Immediately I was flooded with support.

So when the founding members and original attendees started to go in different life directions, the group looked like it was going to end for good. I had been still very new to the group, but I believed in what it was doing so strongly, it couldn't end. This is where my beginning of my company came from literally, it needed to live on to help support other women in any type of business.

Wendy, Nancy, Melissa, Beth and I brainstormed because we each felt so strongly in the mission. We decided to keep it going. We would rename the group to WINGS (Women Inspiring Networking Giving and Supporting). This could open it up to women who didn't necessarily have a business, but wanted connection, as I saw so many women I worked with did. We would continue WINGS one weeknight a month. We would collect dues and 100% would go to a charity we agreed on together. We would adopt a local family at Christmas. We tried to do as much good as we could, supporting each other and our community. In the beginning, there might have been a handful of us, but we believed so strongly in the concept that we continued. The group then grew and grew, at the highest peak we probably had about 30 women with us. All sorts of backgrounds, women who needed that connection and support! We had each other's back, that's for sure.

Through all of this I was growing and growing as a person and would soon grow into the person everyone would turn to if they had a need. I always dove in to help. People would call me "the connector." Huh?? I didn't see myself like that. I had no clue what they were talking about, I mean most of my WINGS and WIP friends were avid readers in everything self-help, motivational, and business oriented. So according to Malcolm Gladwell and my friends I was "the connector." I had connections all over the board, on every level, and just about any situation. This became a great gift for me and for others. Being able to connect people for various reasons has helped me greatly both personally and professionally. What a gift it is to put people who need each other for whatever reason together. If only I could do that with my love life, I'd be all set! That's another book entirely.

But just by being aware and paying attention, we're able to support one another. So that's what I try to do, just listen. People come to me because sometimes they are not comfortable in putting themselves out there. We've already established that I don't have an issue there, so they ask me to help them. As long as I believe in what's going on, why the heck not? From full-time employment, finding furniture, selling items, moving people, cookie ladies, recycling, authors, charities, CEO's, to people in need. I run the gamut and can connect you to most any resource locally and some even not so locally. It's sure a change from the quiet one many years ago to finding my true voice in my 30's. Here I am. It's never too late, ladies, to open up to who you were born to be.

Seizing Opportunity and Rising Together

Now, while all this was occurring and even years before, I had this burning desire to create a women's group not for business or networking but for women to just connect. I was thinking maybe to meet once a month and to do a travel retreat 2 times a year. So many women I spoke to wanted to do something like this, they just didn't have anyone to join them. I wanted to change all that personally.

At the time I was working with a very kind women named Megan, we grew very close while organizing her house. She was very bright and creative. I had shared my idea at some point and she wholeheartedly believed in it. So much so, that she wanted to be a part of it. She was doing research and even coming up with company names. It was amazing. Someone saw my vision and wanted in. I believed I needed a partner to do something so massive. I saw my client and friend Moira run a very successful triathlon women's group of over 600 members and each member just adored her. So why couldn't I?

Ultimately Megan and I did not go any further with the idea. I left my notebook full of ideas there in my complimentary free Lancôme purple bag, that moved with me a few times and resided in the back bottom of my closet. I would not revisit that notebook until the day after Jenn and I hosted our first SOAR Women's Symposium event in 2017, a good five years later.

What is SOAR, you ask? S.O.A.R stands for Seize Opportunity and Rise, and it is a bi-annual Women's Symposium. Two times per year, we bring together 100 women for a day to share, connect, learn, and grow together. Let me back up a bit. Jenn (the author who asked me to speak at BOLDHER) out of the blue one day in 2015 had asked me if we could talk. I mean we talked regularly, but for some reason this felt different. What could this be about it? It sounded kind of important. So we set a time to talk over the phone.

"Jess, you know how important BOLDHER was to so many women? I'd like to bring it closer to our home, on the Jersey Shore. Not BOLDHER exactly, but something like it. Would you be interested in being my partner?" All I could think of at the time is what an honor, Jenn knew so many incredible women. I was just little old me, nothing too special about me. Why on earth did she want me? Sure I enjoyed helping people, but this was big time!!

So did I know what being her partner meant, no not really. Did either one of us have tons, if any disposable income or capital to start this thing? Absolutely not. Jenn just went through a massive financial mess, and I was a single mom with no child support. Of course we could start another venture together! I said "Yes" with my heart racing.

My head immediately went into planning mode. I made lists, organized information, and got right on it. Jenn and I made an appointment to go see the historic Berkeley Carteret in Asbury Park. We toured this amazing location with 7 different room options at that time. By that time I was researching busing options because nobody would want to pay for the parking meter for all those hours. I made list after list on everything I could possibly think of, sending Jenn endless Google documents. The Berkeley sent us pricing, and all of this seemed to add up dollars wise. But I still was ready like a bull charging through.

Something began to change. I wasn't hearing from Jenn as much, and sometimes there was a sort of radio silence. Things felt off, so I loosened the reins. I didn't realize that Jenn often followed the direction that came through in her prayer and meditation. And she knew although it would be something, now was not the time. She didn't want to pull the plug on it until she was certain it wasn't just her own fear holding her back.

Eventually, Jenn and I talked, and she had the courage to open her heart to me and tell me with some degree of difficulty that it didn't feel like the right time. I had to respect her feelings, and just trust that it wasn't meant to be, at least not at that time. I certainly didn't want to take on that huge endeavor alone, I mean it wasn't even my idea. So I let it go. It wasn't easy. By that time I had done a lot of work and research. I was so excited and honored, but sometimes things just don't work out the way you want them to.

So that was the end of that story. We were friends, but the topic didn't resurface until 2 years later. Yes, you heard that right. At that time the women's conference was a thought long ago that kind of just went away for me.

Then sometime in the early spring of 2017, Jenn calls me and says, "Can we talk?" This was a different tone, and I almost knew what might be coming. Would she really want to try out this women's conference again on the Jersey Shore? So in the days between I was preparing myself with ideas and questions for if in fact this was what Jenn wanted to talk about. There was still a tad bit of unresolved pain and hurt for the letdown of the work I had done. I am a jumper, a doer, a get in and goer. I was hurt she didn't get in and go with me, even after she explained why! I mean not so hurt we weren't friends but concerned enough to be skittish. But if there's one thing I've now learned from Jenn, sometimes we need to take a beat and listen to God's direction.

When Jenn and I did talk, I was ready. Jenn told me she had a dream and woke up with the words "Seize Opportunity and Rise" in her heart. When she wrote it down, she realized the initials came out to S.O.A.R.

When we talked in 2015, we couldn't agree on a name. She kept saying Spark, Bounce, Soar but I didn't love that. I liked the word "soar" but not the rest. All of a sudden, four little words gave me the biggest chills. It was like I heard the alarm clock going off. It was time. She expressed that she felt that this was the message of the dream, that the time to put together this women's conference we'd spoken about years prior had come, and that time was now. If felt so good but I was still a tad bit guarded. I did ask Jenn, if she was really sure this time. I dive head first and deep into projects. I'm pretty relentless and I didn't want to do that again unless it was for real. She said, "Yes," and even said she would do the legwork since she knew how much time I'd put into it years before. I knew she meant it, and I believed her.

In the Spring of 2017, our financial situations had not improved all that much, for me it might have even been worse. I'm pretty sure at that time my child support was completely MIA. Although I did have one credit card with a few thousand dollars as the limit and I would offer to use that because I believed wholeheartedly in the mission. Jenn believed we wouldn't have to go that route. She said God gave us the dream,

He will provide the resources. It was a good balance—Jenn being a huge believer and me the more practical one in a sense. So again I believed her. She seemed to have a direct connection to the man upstairs. And I like that it was the whole, "If you build it they will come" kind of thing. Anything that comes out of Jenn's mouth literally feels like you can totally do it, and with total trust, too. Over the years, I've hoped to be more like that, I mean just how amazing to think like that.

So Jenn and I made appointments to go see 2 locations in Pier Village, Long Branch. I mean you couldn't get any closer to the shore than that. My girlfriend Amanda worked at the high-end restaurant, and rooftop lounge, so I reached out to her and she set up the appointment. Then Jenn and I would go over to the Bungalow Hotel. Let's just say the minute we walked up those beautiful wide-open, wooden stairs with floor to ceiling windows looking out at the Atlantic Ocean, we knew this was the spot. This was the moment it felt more than real. Jenn said being surrounded by the ocean represented endless possibilities and our limitless potential. What a gift to give our attendees, right? A subliminal message that you, my friend, are infinite. I even asked our events coordinator about the "dolphin package." He didn't know what the heck I was talking about, so I asked if we could order dolphins to jump out in the water during our event. Joking of course, but seriously how cool would dolphins be?!

The vibe was amazing, the furniture was hip. We were in love but still knowing in the back of our heads this place charges a $150 per person for weddings!! So we continued to walk just a few blocks away to the Bungalow Hotel, not on the ocean. Sure you walk into this ultra-hip lobby, with a ton of fun going on inside. The decor was unique, it was featured on TV but the only space they had would be the lobby. There was just no way around the columns of the room, just too many obstacles, not to mention Jenn and I left our hearts back at the rooftop.

So we powwowed for a bit after our two experiences. This conference would be a huge undertaking, physically, emotionally, and financially. I really knew I'd never done something to this scale and capacity. This was defying all my odds. Jenn with complete faith assured me we could do this, and if we did it right we wouldn't even have to use any money out of pocket. She said it all so clearly. Maybe it was all her previous experience in just about everything, but whatever it was, I believed and jumped in.

Jenn coordinated the contract with the venue, even negotiated no money up front giving us time to get the deposit we needed through ticket sales. She made a save the date, an Eventbrite page to sell tickets, a Facebook page to promote it, and we totally went for it. We began to put together this day for women to connect with each other and take the day for themselves. A day that they so very much deserved, this wouldn't be just another networking event for working women, it was an open door. Stay-at-home moms to CEO's, we welcomed every woman with open arms. It was my hope to give that special warm feeling to women that felt in need of it, whether she knew it or not. We all need a tribe or community, it's a proven fact by the way!

Talk about hitting the ground running. Jenn and I put together everything we needed. Amazing session leaders just showed up in our hearts, and when we asked them they said YES without hesitation or a need to be paid! Jenn built a website and we hustled to sell tickets and get sponsors to cover the deposit. I must have messaged close to a thousand people! If you were one of my Facebook friends and a female, whether I knew you or not, you probably got a message from me. We were moving at lighting speed together, the very first bi-annual SOAR Women's Symposium was happening, and we had just about 6 months to pull it all together.

The women came—the session leaders, the panelists, and attendees, tickets were sold, sponsorship tables were booked, heck even the Girl Scouts of the Jersey Shore came on, it was all coming together. To see all the women that we knew and some we did not, sitting at one super long table together. Somehow they all found us. It was happening!

Fast forward to October 16, 2017, about 5 am our day had started, and yes it was drizzling. The previous night Jenn, Nicole (our attention to detail team member for all the decor), and myself got this magnificent oceanfront space ready. This was happening, we sold all of our tickets and even were able to add just a few more a few days before. Everything was lining up, we had a few hiccups, but we just took a deep breath and powered through them all. Doors opened around 7:30 am and our first attendee coming up those beautiful stairs was my dear friend Antonia. Now she has never been known to be early for anything, but today she was! The women started arriving. Jenn was at check in and it was my job to socialize—seems fair enough, right? Next thing you know there was a commotion going on. Well come to find out the ladies outside on the rooftop deck saw something that many had never seen, even myself living here my entire life.

Can you guess what it might have been??

You got it—a pod of dolphins frolicking merrily directly in front of us! And that was not it. Several breaching whales, I kid you not, were out in the water, too. Never in my life had I ever experienced anything so magical. They stayed with us for about an hour. So when I had jokingly asked our events coordinator for the dolphin package and he laughed it off, the joke was on him because, well that is just what I got. You know that saying, "Be careful of what you ask for because you just might get it," I mean dolphins, whales and a room full of women!!

The day was a smashing success. The lunch was last on the schedule. All 60 women went downstairs and enjoyed a beautiful lunch together in this magnificent light- filled room on the ocean. When I took a moment, I looked around and saw a sea of women, sitting with friends and strangers just enjoying themselves. I will be forever grateful for that image Jenn and I had made come to life with pure faith.

That night and the next day our phones and emails where flooded with kind words, thanks, and appreciation for what that day had done for so many women. So all the blood, sweat, and tears was 100% worth it!

Jenn and I got together the next day to powwow. Sitting in the car in front of Jenn's Wanamassa home, I had an "aha" moment. That women's thing I wanted to create back in 2011, well this was so much like it. I couldn't believe it. I shared this moment with Jenn, and she said back in 2011 she also had this type of idea, and here it took 6 years to birth but we did it together!

Since our first SOAR we are now coming upon our 5th event. Each event is so magnificent and I'm happy to report, we have sold out every year, and have grown slightly each time. From the cliff of the Highlands of the Water Witch Club, to the rustic modern barn on the alpaca farm of Edel Haus to the art gallery Detour in the heart of Red Bank, and the upcoming top floor of the new Wave Resort. Our blessing just running over. It's never easy but it's always been worth it. We have made a pact as a team that we will bring 100 women together every six months so we can connect, share, learn, and grow with one another, and of course Seize Opportunity and Rise Together.

Make It Your Business to Believe in Your Dreams

Honor Your Thoughts

When something comes into your heart or mind, take note of it. Don't brush it aside as if it's no big deal. Your thoughts matter and they give you clues to the things you need to be doing in the world—good ones, not so good ones, they all have hidden messages! Grab a journal and write those thoughts down! Reflect on them and do whatever you can to make something good that serves others out of the ideas that come to you.

Don't Force It, But Don't Forget It

Timing is everything. If you are working on a dream and it's just not coming together no matter what you do or you kind of feel like a bull in a china shop, give that dream a minute. Things should come together a little easier than that. I mean, it always takes work but if you are fighting forces in every direction, maybe the time is not now. But don't tuck that dream so far away that you forget about it. Continue visualizing and take steps towards it that feel more natural. There's no rush! It will happen when it's meant to happen.

No Money? No Problem

... but, be prepared to work your butt off! Seriously, money is only an obstacle if you choose to make it one. It took me many years to learn this one, but the world really is abundant and the money you need will come to you exactly when you need it when you are building a dream that helps others. Don't be afraid to take the steps even if you don't know exactly how or when it will all happen. It helps to break things down to the teeniest tiniest measure, so you just need to get to the first dollar, not the hundred thousandth right away!

It's Not About You But You are Necessary

This is a doozy. Your dream is not about you, but you are the chosen one to fulfill it because the dream came to YOU. Your greatest good gives the courage for others to do their greatest good. When you take a step, you encourage others to take a step, or even just open themselves up to dream. And remember, your dream is supposed to help and serve others. But if you allow it to, you will be served something magical as well!!

Afterword

Your Life is Your Legacy

"The purpose of life is not to be happy. It is to be useful, to be honorable, to be compassionate, to have it make some difference that you have lived and lived well." ~ Ralph Waldo Emerson

A few weeks before our last SOAR Symposium, I had no idea what I was going to speak about. Jenn suggested I talk about "legacy". She knew I created the group "Tami's Legacies" and she also knew everything I work so hard for is to create a legacy, something for my children to be proud of, perhaps carry on. Everything I do is for the four of them, after all.

But, me, talk about legacy? What a big word. The funny thing is, Jenn does this all the time. She notices something or sees something in me, and pushes me way out of my comfort zone. The next thing you know I am standing in front of 100 women talking about legacy. I remember saying, "Legacy is about how we live, not how we die." And while saying that I felt it hard to catch my breath. The words just felt so heavy, so important.

Legacy isn't tomorrow. Legacy is NOW. How people think of you now is how people WILL think of you then. Today is tomorrow's legacy. Every interaction every single day and the way we spend it. Our legacy is in every email we send, ever conversation we have, every call, every text, every action, every reaction... What are yours saying?

Towards the end of 2018, something especially got me thinking about my legacy. There was a horrible plane crash in Africa at that time. One of the guys on the flight had gone to Haiti. I know that because they said it ALOT on the news in describing this man who lost his life. Like a wave coming over me, I had to wonder, what would my legacy be? I hadn't really thought of it.

My father died young, as did my dear friends Tami and Kelly. None of us never really know when it will be our time. How many blessed years will you or I have left? I'm not afraid of aging, growing old. In fact, I welcome it! Grey hair, wrinkles? Yes please and thank you!

As a professional organizer, there's a technique I learned called the Swedish Death Cleaning. The idea is to clean so good before you die so your relatives aren't left going through a bunch of junk. To me, the idea of a death cleaning is to leave a legacy of who you are, not the stuff you leave behind.

"No one is useless in this world who lightens the burdens of another." ~ Charles Dickens

I found this incredible list by Dan Rockwell, "10 Ways to Build a Powerful Legacy". They are:

1. Dare to be joyful. Serve in ways that bring you joy. Angry, unhappy people leave sad legacies.
2. Monitor your impact on others. What are you doing when you make the biggest difference. Do more of that.
3. Develop and maximize your talent, strengths, and skills.
4. Know yourself – Bring yourself.
5. Do what matters now. Everyone who's at the end of life says it goes by fast.
6. Seize small opportunities. Big may follow. Stop waiting to make a difference. Start with those closest to you and the ones you spend the most time with.
7. Bring your best self to work and family. Everyone has at least two selves. Bring out the best one.
8. Think service not success.
9. Relax. Don't run around building a legacy. Run around making a difference.
10. Elevate the needs of others over your own.

How do you measure up with the list? What area can you use a boost with? Do you have tips of your own to add to it? I struggle with relaxing, being still. I am pledging from here on out to work on that. I would like my legacy to be something like......

> *Jessica Varian Carroll was a kind and generous soul, that loved to help others, volunteered often some would say daily, she took chances, threw good parties and events, was a great friend, gave talks about topics that were close to her heart hoping to help others, wrote a killer memoir that hit the New York Times best sellers list, cared a lot about many, founded Organista Home, co founded Soar Symposium and created her first philanthropic foundation all with just a high school degree, raised 4 wonderful children Jared, Noah, Reilly and Damian that are living examples of her honor. Her simple quote was "be good, do good".*

Our legacy should simply be our way of life and helping others. We all create our legacy everyday, I'm curious - what's yours? Are you actively creating it? If not, Begin living deliberately with intention. Make it your business to live your legacy starting now...

In the space below, write your legacy and read it daily. Take actions in total alignment with the legacy you've written below.

Acknowledgements

This book would not have come together without the love and support of so many amazing people.

To my children, The Carroll Clan, we've been through it all, and I've always tried to be the best role model to show you the sky's the limit and anything is possible. But it's you guys who have taught me strength, resilience, and unconditional love. Jared my pied piper, mayor, hustler, big things in store for you! Noah, my gentle giant, the quick witted funny one, and can't forget what a great dancer you are, you are capable of so much more than you know! Reilly, you've got brains, beauty, ambition, and all I can say is watch out world! Damian, my kind, sweet, and athletic "D", I can only imagine the mark you will leave. Thank you all beyond words! I couldn't have done this (or anything) without you.

To my parents for your belief in kindness and your strong faith. You are such good people, and you have supported me through the good, the bad, and the ugly.

Mom, thank you, including passing down your organizational skills and selflessness to others, especially those down on their luck. Your humble way in the world provided me a great example through your actions and care for people.

Who would I possibly be without you? And Dad, my hard working father, thank you for always keeping a smile on your face, and of course for your killer dance moves. ps I love you and miss you Dad.

To Tara and Timmy for always going along with all my crazy shenanigans and always being in my corner even when it's outside your comfort zone - I'm so very grateful!

To my nephew and Godson, Keiran - I'm so proud of everything you've done and accomplished. I'm just in awe of your gifts.

To my nephew and Godson, Baby Roman welcome to the world, it's all yours! I love seeing life through those big blue eyes and your loving heart.

To my longest and dearest friends Amy and Lesly - we've been through it all. I'm so grateful for your listening ears and all of your support always!! Amy since the softball fi elds of the middle school we've been thick as thieves. Lesly since high school you've been here for me, so grateful for our daily chats and you jumping in to help, just about always!

To my dear friends in Heaven that were taken far too soon Tami and Kelly. I think of you guys often. Your lives and deaths have both taught me so much. I'm forever grateful and will see you up there one day.

To Melissa—thank you so much for choosing me to be your Godmother even if I had to twist your arm a bit. It's been such a blessing to see you grow into the beautiful woman you are today.

To Kirsten, Phil, John, Chris, Monica, Dorothy, Stephen,

Maria, and Teresa, my extended children - your hearts are beyond magnificent. I'm so proud of each and everyone of you. Your strength and courage is something to be admired. I know your mother Tami is shining through each of you.

To Veera thank you for taking a chance on me so many years ago! Client #1. Thank you for always believing in me even the times I just couldn't see it, for your incredible wisdom you have always so generously given to me and keeping me going in my harder days. I'd be lost without you. You are my rock!

To Natalie, you are a true friend, always there to jump in, even if it takes a little arm twisting! You are a supporter, and you have a such a gift of words that blesses me through every conversation, toast, and written word we exchange.

To my very extended tribe, from near, far, and wide, each and everyone of you mean so much to me. Always pitching in, supporting and with such loyalty. You are the reason I keep going and putting myself out there, it's all because of you. You guys rock!

To Jenn not sure where to begin, well first I'm sure this book wouldn't have come to light without you! I'm so glad we crossed paths so many years ago because since then my life has shifted to an even greater capacity to be able to help others. Your true selflessness has been a gift to witness. Can't stop, won't stop! We got this! Partners for life!

To anyone reading this book, wow. I hope it has impacted you in some small way, that you may have found even just a small nugget in these words. I am grateful you took a shot and bought a book written by little old me. It means so much and my hope is you realize that whatever the world says you have no business doing, whenever the world says you can't do something, you show them heck yeah, you definitely can!!

xoxo Jessica

Stay in Touch

To connect with Jessica online, visit:
http://shehadnobusiness.com

To learn more about Organista Home, visit
http://organistahome.com

To attend a S.O.A.R Women's Symposium, visit
http://seizeopportunityandrise.com

To join the conversation and share all the awesome things you have no business doing, but do anyway, use hashtag #shehadnobusiness.